JIM

P9-DNI-856

I'M GLAD
YOU DIDN'T
TAKE IT
PERSONALLY

Edited by LEONARD SHECTER

A DELL BOOK

Published by
DELL PUBLISHING CO., INC.
750 Third Avenue
New York, New York 10017

Reprinted by arrangement with
William Morrow and Company, Inc.
New York, New York

Printed in the United States of America

First Dell printing—February 1972
Second Dell printing—April 1972
Third Dell printing—May 1972

CONTENTS

Dedication   1

1. The Tube and I   5

2. The Last Great Half Season
   of J. Bouton   41

3. The King and I   70

4. Sanctity of the Clubhouse   85

5. Telling It Like It Isn't   99

6. The Subject Is Roses—
   and Daffodils   139

7. Advertisements for Myself   154

8. Sweet and Sour Mash Notes   169

9. Writing Books for Fun and Profit   184

10. The Making of a Social Leper   200

11. Return of the Native   218

12. The Game I Love   229

"I feel sorry for Jim Bouton. He is a social leper. He didn't catch it, he developed it. His collaborator on the book, Leonard Shecter, is a social leper. People like this, embittered people, sit down in their time of deepest rejection and write. They write, oh hell, everybody stinks, everybody but me, and it makes them feel much better."—Dick Young, reviewing *Ball Four* in the New York *Daily News*, May 28, 1970.

I saw Dick Young the next day in the visitors' clubhouse at Shea Stadium in New York. I guess if I had been the kind of player he liked I'd have offered him a punch in the mouth. I mean, what would Roger Maris have done if Dick Young called *him* a social leper? If he had done it to Denny McLain I suppose he'd have gotten a bucket of ice water over his head. Me, I just shot him a little wave, and I could feel this dumb grin spreading over my face. I didn't feel angry. I didn't even think he stank.

"Hi Jim," Dick Young said.

"Hi Dick," I said. "I didn't know you were talking to social lepers these days."

Dick Young is probably the most famous and most likely the best baseball writer in the country. He is certainly the elder statesman of his craft. Also he has this jutting jaw, and even though his hair is all gray now, he has a pugnacious personality that has not been softened by the years. Dick Young can still sound like gangbusters just by asking the time. But at this point the drawn, nervous look on his face turned into a tight little smile. "Well," he said, *I'm glad you didn't take it personally.*" I think the italics are mine.

No, I didn't take it personally. Because I never felt rejected, never believed I had written *Ball Four* out of any sense of retribution. In fact, I didn't know what the hell Dick Young was talking about. (As for my collaborator, Leonard Shecter, all I can say about him is that he laughs a lot these days.) The only thing I feel toward Dick Young now is gratitude. I believe it was his overreaction to *Ball Four* as well as the overreaction of hundreds of sports writers, columnists, telecasters, and one of my main men, Bowie Kuhn, the Commissioner of Baseball, which helped make the book a best seller; so successful, if I may say so with unaccustomed immodesty, that it sold more hardcover copies than any sports book in the recorded history of the English-speaking world.

And so, because of the astonishingly great help they have been, it is to Dick Young and Bowie Kuhn and those other faceless heroes of the bloody war to protect America from the small truths about baseball revealed in *Ball Four* that I respectfully dedicate this book. I hope they don't take it personally.

1.

THE TUBE AND I

The only pitching I do now is on television. I didn't plan it that way.

It was, I admit, in the back of my mind for a long time. I do not consider this a particularly noble or terribly exclusive ambition. There is hardly a professional athlete in America who, casting about for some easy way to make a living once his athletic skills have abandoned him, doesn't think television. It looks so easy.

There are, naturally enough, few players who come out of the game with a doctorate in electrical engineering. So you look around and think, "Now what can I do?" Read scores, that's what. *Anybody* can read scores—for a minute and a half anyway. The job is easy, the pay is good, the hours short, the fame instant. All of those unworthy thoughts, I admit, crept easily through my greedy mind.

I knew, though, it wasn't going to be that simple for me. It might be simple for a Kyle Rote or a Frank Gifford. These guys were big national figures. They brought a lot of fame to their television jobs plus good looks of a kind that women respond to with, at the very least, dewy eyes. It's no accident that Frank Gifford is the new Betty Furness of the airwaves.

I was missing a lot of the ingredients. There was a small measure of fame in winning thirty-nine games plus two in the World Series for the Yankees in 1963 and 1964. But what had I done lately? Besides, I never saw myself as turning women dewy. I mean I don't think I'm ugly; at the same time I'm hardly a matinee idol. I have rather narrow, deeply set eyes, and for some odd reason my friend Gary Bell, who used to be a pitcher too, calls me Ass Eyes.

Given all the combinations and limitations, I made a realistic conclusion: radio. When I'm through with baseball I'll take this little radio job with a small New Jersey station. Although it wouldn't pay much, I wouldn't care. I'd take it for the experience. I'd work at it for a few years, see if I liked it, see if it liked me. With that experience, plus the advantage of having been a Yankee, I could probably get a job on a local TV station, something small, again for a small amount of money. And so on, up and away, until after ten years or so I might land a job with a New York station. That's what I thought.

Then all of a sudden I got sexy. There are a lot of ways to do that in television. You could, for example, be a Caucasian-looking black female reporter twenty-five years old with fifteen years of experience in the media. That's very sexy indeed. Another way is to be an athlete who writes a best seller. That's me.

The book was barely out when I got a call from Al Primo, who is News Director of Channel 7, ABC news, in New York. Would I be interested in a television job? Well, er, yes. Fine. We'd talk about it during the All-Star break and if everything worked out I could quit baseball and start on the tube right away.

Gulp.

In New York at the All-Star break I did an audition. It was terrible. Part of the problem was that I didn't know what the hell I was doing. The other part was that they had prepared some stuff for me to read. The material was full of "lackluster performances" and "vaunted attacks" and "heralded righthanders." I kept stumbling over these brilliant phrases. I thought I'd blown it. I really did.

Later I found out why I hadn't. Primo's wife. She'd seen me on the Dick Cavett show. Or maybe the David Frost show. She said, "Al, he'll work."

And he said, "I go along with my wife's instincts."

("One thing about Primo," my producer, Art Browne, was to tell me later on. "He has an innate ability to pick raw talent.")

So Primo offered me a job, a five-year contract

7

to do sports for Eyewitness News, ABC's New York news show. Salary: $40,000 to start, going to $50,000, with the possibility of additional network wherewithal. It was tempting as hell. I was making $27,000 with the Houston Astros. It meant being home instead of on the road. It meant the start of a new and challenging, not to mention lucrative, career. It also meant quitting baseball right away. So I said no.

Al Primo gave me a very funny look. So did Ken MacQueen, vice-president and general manager, who was also in the office. I mean they liked *Ball Four* because it was irreverent and funny and that's what they wanted me to bring to Channel 7. But they didn't know I was *crazy*.

MacQueen went to work on me. People don't get opportunities like this. It could be the most important thing that ever happened to me in my whole life. Did I realize what other men, big men in athletics, would give to have that job?

I said yeah, I know. I'm crazy. But I had a reason. I didn't want to work those kinds of hours. It would have meant being away from home from about noon until midnight, five days a week. It would have meant running around like a maniac with a microphone in my hand. That's worse than baseball. I'd *never* see my kids. I said that was my reason. Actually it was my excuse. I simply wasn't ready to leave baseball. Even after the Houston Astros sent me down, I still thought I could pitch.

So did Manager Harry Walker. At least that's what he said. "I still think you have a future," Harry said when he gave me my papers to Oklahoma City. This was in August, more than a month after I'd said no to ABC. "You know, you showed a good fastball from time to time. I think your arm is getting stronger and I think you can have a good year next year. We're not outrighting you to Oklahoma City. We're only optioning you out. We can get you back anytime."

I believed.

I even believed when I pitched badly in my first game for Oklahoma City (six innings, six runs). And I believed after I got knocked out in the first inning of my next start. Six runs in the first, and the Indianapolis Indians beat the Oklahoma City Eighty-niners, 9–2. What a way to go.

Singles by such superstars as Ron Theobald, Jay Warden and Don Anderson started it. Then Elvio Jiminez hit a home run. Bill Plummer was up next and I hit him in the ribs with a pitch. The Indianapolis guys were pissed off at me because they thought I was throwing at him. They couldn't have been reading my stuff. This particular author has revealed he doesn't throw at people. I did try to brush him back, though. Instead, I hit him. Shows what great control I had.

Then Kurt Bevacqua gained undying fame by hitting another home run, and when the manager, a man who was actually named Hub Kittle, came to get me, I almost said, "What kept you?" So Kurt Bevacqua was the last man to get a hit off me in organized baseball. *That's* something to tell his grandchildren. Not that I knew it at the time. I was still hanging on, finding excuses. I hadn't been getting enough work. The knuckleball is erratic. I'm erratic. My head isn't on straight. My uniform wasn't tight enough. When you want to kid yourself, you find a lot of ways to do it.

In the end, I sat down and wrote a list of pros and cons. You know, like the reasons for going into Cambodia and for not going in. The only thing that was on the pro side was that I liked playing baseball. I didn't want to face having to leave it. When you do something for so long, it becomes a way of life. It's damned hard to leave something you know for something you don't know.

Decisions are not made so coolly and logically, however. I believe decisions about your life are made viscerally, almost unconsciously. And a few things did happen. . . .

After losing that second game for Oklahoma City, I didn't go on with the club to Indianapolis. I had made commitments for book-signings in San Francisco when I got there with the Houston club. Of course, I wasn't going to be there with the Houston club. I got permission to go anyway.

On the way to San Francisco I took the opportunity to stop off in Seattle, the scene for most of *Ball Four*. A press conference was arranged. I hit some local radio shows. For most of a day, I was the toast of Seattle. It was even better to be the toast of San Francisco. I spent the whole day there walking the hills, signing books, appearing on everybody's radio and TV show. I really felt like a big deal.

The next day I was at the tiny airport in Evansville, Indiana. Evansville goddam Indiana. When the plane landed the weather was drippy and muggy and depressing. The hotel was called the McCurdy, and when I went up to my room I found it was tiny and cramped. Lying there on one of the little beds was a nineteen-year-old rookie in his shivvies watching TV. So I stripped to my underwear and lay down to watch TV with him.

I was looking at the TV, half wondering whether the game would be called, thinking about being a big man in Seattle and San Francisco and about being in this goddam hotel in Evansville, when I happened to look down on the bedspread and there was a large spot of dried blood on it. "Hey, what's this blood?" I said to the kid. "How'd it get here?"

And he said, "Ah, she must have been having her period."

"Who must have been having her period?"

11

"The broad they were fucking last night."

Jesus. I'm glad they were nice enough to keep the bedcover on. And there was this little click in my mind. . . .

Columbia, South Carolina. I'm nineteen years old, a Yankee rookie, and tomorrow is going to be the first day of my first spring training. I'm standing outside the Jerome Hotel in Columbia, South Carolina, at about eleven o'clock at night. It's an hour before curfew and I plan to stand there in the street, just looking around. A guy drives up in a big Cadillac, leans out and says, "You one of the ballplayers?"

I tell him yeah, and it feels good to be able to say it.

"Well, listen," the guy says. "One of the owners is having a party for the players and I'm helping him round them up. He wants to introduce you to some of the people in town." So I jump in.

Another mistake.

The next thing I know we're parked on a road in the woods and I'm contending with what we intellectuals call a homosexual confrontation. My first.

No, I don't feel I want to punch him in the mouth. What I feel toward him mostly is sympathy. Yes, I'm sorry for the poor bastard. For the rest, I'm scared. I can just see the headlines: YANKEE ROOKIE INVOLVED IN SEX CRIME. I don't know what to do. I don't want to make the guy

angry and I don't want to hit him, but for crissakes, he's got my shirt pulled up and he's poking
his fingers into my belly.

"Sir, I'm just not ready for that," I say cleverly,
edging away. "I'm sorry, it doesn't seem as though
I'd enjoy that." I try to be nice about it and pretty soon we're into this long philosophical discussion about right, wrong and sex and I decide I've
got him talked out of it. Wrong again. All of a
sudden he's moving closer. And I have to say,
"Look, if you don't take me back to the hotel right
now, I don't want to do it, but I'm going to have
to punch you out." Understand, I'm not sure I
can make myself do it. I think probably I can't.
But I say it anyway. Fortunately, he believes.

After he drops me off at my hotel I go right up
to my room, still sweating. When I get there,
there's a line of guys outside the door and the
one in front is looking through the keyhole. Since
it is my room, I get to go to the head of the line.
And when I look into the room, there's my roommate and a local talent on the bed. My bed.

Now here I am, eleven years later, in Evansville goddam Indiana, with blood on my bedspread. There was a great sense of déjà vu. This
is where I came in.

The game was called that night in Evansville
and I went out to eat—alone. On my way back
from the restaurant I passed a big auditorium in
which a shitkicking country-western folk music

concert featuring Merle Haggard was on. Since it was intermission, I was able to drift into the auditorium without buying a ticket. And there we were, me and the shitkickers, me keeping time. The next morning I called Primo to find out if the job was still open. He said it was. (Later on he told me that while he and MacQueen thought I was crazy, they also thought that I'd be back. So they stopped looking.) Then I called Bobbie, my wife, in Houston, and told her to pack. We were going home.

In the coffee shop the next morning at the McCurdy I ran into Jim Duffalo and Danny Osinski and sat down to breakfast with them. There we were, three old-time righthanders, reminiscing. Right away we started kidding each other about our magnificent careers. Duffalo said he never remembered Osinski doing very much and Osinski said, oh, yeah, what about the World Series he pitched in? What World Series, we said, pretending not to remember. (It was with Boston in 1967, but we made him tell us.) Then Duffalo said *he* had been in a World Series, too, and now he had us. We really didn't know which one. It was when he was with the Giants, who played against the Yankees in 1962. Duffalo and I were both there. Neither of us got into a game.

Then they both started talking about how this was their last year and how they weren't coming back next year, because this was no life and there was no money in it anymore. Osinski said he was going to work in a bank and Duffalo was going to do this or that, and I kept looking into their faces and thinking, there I am, nine or ten years from now. I knew these guys had said the same thing to themselves last August over breakfast and the August before, and there they were now, both forty or pushing it, and still kidding themselves. If they quit ten years ago, maybe they could have built themselves some kind of business, another life.

Ah, I don't know. Who the hell am I to say? Maybe they got something out of staying in baseball. Maybe it was right for them, everything including the promises to quit each year. Me, I was thirty-one, and I was through. I never even told them. I thought maybe they'd resent it.

I went up to Hub Kittle's room to tell him my decision. He's an old pitcher and he's been in baseball all his life. He tried to talk me out of quitting. "Oh Jimmy, Jimmy, don't quit now, not just because you've had a couple of bad games," he said. "We're going to give you another start. Tomorrow night you're pitching in relief and maybe one more time after that and then I'm going to start you. Jimmy, if you leave this game, you'll be sorry. I'm telling you, it'll be the biggest mistake you ever made. Because, Jimmy, you're going to want to get back into this game. It was the same with me. You know, I'm the only pitcher that ever played over a period of four decades.

15

And I'm going to get into a game here late in the season and it'll be five decades."

My heart went out to the old man. It was as though he was leaving the game and I was trying to talk him into staying. But I couldn't help thinking, "Fame comes to Hub Kittle."

"Jimmy, I'm telling you," he went on, "you're making a mistake. If you leave the game now, you're going to be sorry for the rest of your life. You just feel bad because you've had a couple of bad games. Jimmy, I've seen a lot of guys who felt that way. But do this for me, Jimmy. Sleep on it. Wait a day, sleep on it and then decide."

"I *have* slept on it," I said. "It's not a hasty decision."

"Well, I hate to see you do it," Hub Kittle said. "But if I can't talk you out of it, that's it. I'll call Houston and tell them."

"Thanks, Hub," I said. I stuck my hand out. He shook it. I turned and walked out the door.

I always thought it would be harder than that.

Everybody asks how my kids reacted. A year or so ago there wouldn't have been any reaction at all. Kids don't think much about baseball. But in the last year, particularly the time at Houston, they began to notice that I wasn't just like all other daddies. Especially my oldest, Mike, who's seven now. He'd reached the point where he'd poke me in the ribs when we were sitting around

16

the pool in Houston and say, "Dad, go tell them who you are."

And one day Mike came home from school with a story about a kid who'd been bad and had been called in by the principal. "Dad, he had to go down to the manager's office," Mike said.

When I got the word to report to Oklahoma City, I called the kids together to tell them that I had been sent to the minor leagues. Dave said, "How long are you going to be gone?" And Mike said, "Well, now you can help that team. Can I go along so I can see Mike Marshall's kids?" And little Laurie said, "Dad, will you play monster with me?"

I thought one of the sweet things was said by Mike. "It doesn't matter," he said. "Whether you're playing for the Astros or the Oklahoma team, you're still the same father."

That really touched me, and the next day I said to him, "You know, Mike, what you said to me yesterday was one of the nicest things anybody ever said."

And Mike said, "What did I say?"

"You know, you told me that I was a good father no matter what team I played on."

And Mike said, "I didn't say a good father. I said the *same* father."

Finally there's this bit. The kids always wanted to have a cat or a dog or a turtle or a frog or something as a pet. And I'd always told them they couldn't, because I was a baseball player and we had to travel a lot and you couldn't travel if you had a dog or a cat or a frog, or several of each. So when I returned to Houston from Oklahoma City, I announced to the kids that we were finished with baseball and we were going home to New Jersey.

"Good," they said. "Now we can have a dog."

They said it almost together. Kids know what's important.

The job I settled on with Primo was the eleven o'clock news only—for $24,000; less money for less work, and a one-year contract. They could have insisted on five years, I suppose. However, after watching the mess I made of the audition, I guess they decided to go conservative. There has to be a limit to Primo's faith in his wife's intuition.

It's strange, but the more I work in television, the more I come to see how little different it is from baseball. It might well be that all businesses are the same and that baseball and television, despite the aura of glamour, are just two more. Still, there were some uncanny things.

Take Primo. As News Director he is virtually the prototypic baseball general manager. As Roger Grimsby, who is the growling anchor man of Eyewitness News, has said, Primo is a man who can hear a $5 bill hit the snow. (In baseball, there wasn't a general manager who couldn't have grabbed it before it landed.)

Look, I *like* Primo. He's an amusing guy. And he showed great intelligence, perspicacity and guts when he hired me. Also, he has a terrific wife. Not only that, you have to give him credit for ABC news knocking hell out of NBC and CBS in the ratings. That's like winning a goddam pennant. But, like baseball general managers, he's got some amusing idiosyncrasies.

The Channel 7 blazers. He must have invented them because he insists that the "team" wears them all the time. Like he's the general and the privates shouldn't be out of uniform. In baseball they told me to wear my hat. In television I wear my blazer. One day John Schubeck, who is our revolutionary in residence, showed up without his blazer (blue, a yellow Channel 7 on the breast pocket, right over the heart). At times like that Primo is likely to walk out the door on the way to his car with his hands raised to the sooty sky in deep prayer: "Why are you whipping me?" he implores. "Why are you beating my brains out?"

We never know the answer he gets, but the night after Schubeck forgot his blazer there was a note on his desk signed by Primo. It said: "Schubeck, if I ever see you again without your Channel 7 jacket on, I will hurt you real bad." So far, Schubeck has been shaping up. I can't wait for the next time he misses.

Also like baseball general managers, Primo feels it is necessary to run the private lives of his "team." Everybody gets this speech on divorce.

Primo says he is very "skeptical" about divorce. "Never go all the way with a newsman who has left his wife," Primo always says. "They're basically quitters, and besides, it's a sin."

If Primo gets wind of marital trouble, the newsman is called in for The Talk. It's supposed to save the marriage. Mostly it doesn't, but I suspect Primo feels good for having tried.

One of the first things Primo said to me once I came to work was, "How are things at home? I'm not going to find you and your wife spread all over the *Daily News*, am I?"

"Give me time, Al," I said. "I've just started in this business."

The other Primo lecture has to do with loyalty. Not coming to work prepared is disloyal. Taking too long to shoot a film story is disloyal. Saying bad things on the air is disloyal. Not getting a haircut is disloyal.

I thought it might be disloyal to put all this in a book, but Primo said not at all. His eyes shone. "I'd *love* to be in the book," he said.

Okay, Al.

I also have to tell about the crawl machine. When I first came to Channel 7 I told all concerned that I did not want to read scores. Frank Gifford and those guys can read scores if they want to, but I think it's a bloody waste of time. I agreed to give the local results only, on the ground that nobody cares about the Phoenix-Miami score except some insomniac gamblers.

I'd rather do some kind of interview or editorial swifty. And I got a lot of yassuh bosses from the troops. Except every once in a while, here came the scores. They came on a crawl machine. You've seen them. Background shot of the sport involved. Crawling over the background, the scores. And I'm supposed to read them, just in case the viewers can't.

So I'd fight and win and the crawl machine would be back in the corner and then, all of a sudden, there it would be in front of me again. Finally I found out why. MacQueen is Primo's boss and he spent $3,500 for the crawl machine. So there was, naturally, a lot of pressure from Primo to use it. I think I got it put away permanently now. Can't be sure, though. On the Astros we thought that about the Exergenie, Houston's isometric contraption, from time to time. We were always wrong. The Exergenie cost a lot too.

Another way television is like baseball is that it always invites more guys to spring training than can make the team. Although there is a bit more secrecy involved in television, you find out. And the list of people who tried out for or were offered the job I eventually got is staggering.

Jerry Kramer, another author. Kramer blew it when he took Primo into his chauffeur-driven limousine, explained how rich he was, how many businesses he was involved in and how willing he was to jet into New York a couple or three times a week. He impressed Primo so much, dazzling with his shiny Super Bowl wristwatch and twinkling Super Bowl ring, that he asked himself: "Why the hell does he need ABC?" Primo didn't like his own answer.

Other guys who were given a look were Joe Morrison of the football Giants; Bob Anderson, who used to play for Army; Joe Belino, once of Annapolis; Terry Brennan, former Notre Dame coach; Bill Toomey, the decathlon man, and Jack Kemp, the Buffalo quarterback who went to Congress. Some were turned down, some didn't want the job. Kemp, as Al Primo said, caught Potomac fever. Sam Huff, of middle lineback fame, was a coach for Vince Lombardi in Washington when he was asked and said no. As soon as George Allen was hired after Lombardi died, Huff was on the phone to Primo, inquiring after his health. Primo played with him like a cat with a ball of twine. "What are you doing these days?" Primo kept asking. Sam, suddenly jobless, tried to talk about other things.

"What are you doing these days?" Primo would say. He couldn't have been that interested. He'd already hired one J. Bouton. Television, like back-of-the-bus, can be a rough business.

Then Joe Pepitone. Yessir, the famous hairpiece model, ex of the Yankees, ex of the Astros and, as of this writing at least, not yet ex of the Chicago Cubs.

Pepitone showed up with an "adviser," a cigar-smoking, pinky-ring type. "Look, we just wanna do what's best for Joe here, you unnerstan'," he kept saying. "We wanna keep him in the lime-light, ya know what I mean?"

His audition didn't work. I'm not sure it was Pepitone's fault. Most television screens aren't big enough to get all of Joe's hairpiece into the picture. And then there was his New York accent. Me, I *like* it. Primo, he didn't like it. Nobody is perfect.

Not even Pepitone. In order that the audition shouldn't be a total loss, they asked him what he thought about this fellow J. Bouton. "A prick," Joe Pepitone said. "A real prick."

As George Vecsey of *The New York Times* once wrote, "Peace, Joe Pep. You never meant anyone any harm."

Then we have the matter of the rookie taking over the job of the veteran. That doesn't sit too well, in baseball or television or, I suppose, the Russian Army. The man in question here was Lou Boda, a good broadcaster with a lot of experience. There was nothing intrinsically wrong with the way Boda presented his nightly minute and a half of sports. He took sports seriously (and unquestioningly), was convinced he ought to cram as much information and as many scores into his allotted time as possible. He didn't make any jokes, he didn't smile, he didn't probe. He was told, more than once, to try to be more free-swinging, to laugh it up a bit. And he must have noticed this *parade* of people coming in for auditions. The handwriting was on the wall. Boda wouldn't, or couldn't, read it.

A great many people still believe that news, even sports news, should be all gloom and doom. (Murray Kempton, the essayist and a man I admire, called me "a sophomore comedian" in the *New York Review of Books*.) But Channel 7 and Primo are changing things. The new image is teamwork, laughter, irreverence (and some very solid reporting besides, I ought to add). Television is, after all, show biz. Why shouldn't the news be show biz too? Anyway, somebody out there must have liked what Channel 7 was doing because NBC and CBS were soon trailing in the ratings game and looking around for friendly, irreverent, funny news people. So it goes.

In the process, Lou Boda was moved out in favor of J. Bouton. Boda, I was told later, had a difficult time explaining to his kids why he no longer appeared on the tube. It was a sad story and even old flint-hearted anchor-man Grimsby admitted he was moved. He wasn't the only one. Two weeks after I began at Channel 7 I stopped off at Chipp's Pub, a local watering spot where a lot of us loosen up before the show, and Bill Aylward, one of the Eyewitness News team (WE LIKE EACH OTHER, the ads say), cornered me. "Bouton," he said, "you better shape up. Your stuff is terrible. You're not doing the job, and if

24

you don't get a helluva lot better real fast, you're gone."

I thanked him for his support, which brought out the real reason he was being so friendly. He considered Lou Boda a professional broadcaster and me an interfering, inexperienced, dumb jock. "I don't see why the hell ABC would ever replace Boda with you," he said. "Boda's a pro. He's knowledgeable about sports. He knows the broadcasting business. He's got a lot of friends around here, and if you think you're going to stick, you're wrong. Boda will be back."

I know the argument. In a lot of ways it's a fair one. A guy gives his life to a career in broadcasting and he's replaced by a guy with no experience. Probably it shouldn't be done. And in the case where a broadcaster with some guts is replaced by an establishment-minded, scared ex-athlete who is a fan rather than a reporter, it's an outrage.

But I felt two things here. First of all, I didn't fire anybody personally. ABC was looking to replace Boda. Sooner or later, if it wasn't me, it would have been somebody else. Second, I really felt I was going to bring something to the tube that Boda did not. "Look," I said to Aylward. "Boda gives the sports seriously and straight. Why does it have to be that way? He reads off the scores like they read off the Vietnam battle deaths. You know, sports is not the most important thing that ever happened in the world. I think people want a little humor and some perspective in sports reporting. That's what I'm trying to bring to it. I'm not nearly as professional as I'm going to be six months from now or two years from now. But I'm going to try like hell."

Aylward wasn't impressed. If he'd been running things, I'd have been fired on the spot anyway. (As it is, Channel 7 now gives me three minutes to do my thing. Boda got a lot less.)

There was also, of course, resentment by the particular veteran replaced. Another time in Chipp's Pub somebody asked me one of those sports questions—would the Knicks beat Philadelphia, or what was the score of some game or other—and before I could say anything Lou Boda, who was sitting down the bar a bit, said, loud enough for a lot of people to hear, "He wouldn't know." I let it pass, because I'm cool. Also because I didn't know.

One time, Primo ran into Boda and said, "Hi Lou, how are you?"

He got a very cold look in return.

"Do you really care how I feel?" Boda said. "Do you really?"

"Yeah Lou, I care. I care."

"The hell you do."

End conversation.

Still, like the veteran who has had to become a pinch hitter because of the young pheenom,

Boda came around. I don't think he resents me anymore. In fact, not long ago we got into a liars' poker game in Chipp's. I don't think it hurt any that he won.

As in baseball, too, there's a lot of sex talk around the TV business. It's not as earthy as bullpen sex, but it's omnipresent just the same.

Sample story: This TV news guy is married, although obviously not a fanatic about it. He's got a girl friend, but it's time for a change. The trouble is, breaking up with a girl can be terribly difficult. She cries. Her tears wilt your collar, ruin the press in your suit, maybe even get on your tie. Or she makes a scene, which is terribly undignified. So one day he reads in a book by James Aubrey, former CBS president, that the best way to get rid of a girl is to take her to lunch at a fancy, crowded restaurant and break it to her right there. She'll be too embarrassed to cry, too ashamed to make a scene.

So our newsman takes this girl to Quo Vadis. Posh. Packed with celebrities. The girl is starry-eyed. And he puts it to her right over the Caesar salad. No fooling around. We're through. Whereupon the girl stands up and, in a voice that could be heard on the West Side docks, says, "All you ever wanted to do anyway was fuck, fuck, fuck." She stalks out, every eye in the place on her. And just as she gets to the door, as a parting shot, she turns and hollers, "And you weren't even good at that." The newsman drapes his napkin over his head and sits there for fifteen minutes summoning up enough courage to leave.

Baseball Annies. TV has them too. You could call them TV groupies. You get these calls. And this one actually happened.

NEWSMAN: "Well, would you like to have dinner with me?"

GROUPIE: "Are you married?"

NEWSMAN: "Well, yes."

GROUPIE: "I don't go out to dinner with married men."

NEWSMAN: "How about lunch?"

GROUPIE: "Okay."

And practical jokes. Idle hands do the devil's work, in television as well as baseball. One day I got a letter from a man in the publicity department.

A rumor has come to our attention at the News publicity office which I trust you will be able to quash.

In essence, it is this: several years ago—in the early Sixties, to be more precise—you are said to have visited a fraternity house at Cornell University several times to see your brother. On one of those occasions, you participated in the preparations for a fraternity party by recording a "gag" tape with a fraternity brother named Ernie Steinberg or Steinmetz. The tape is said to have replicated numerous gross and obscene bathroom and outhouse sounds.

The problem is, the other fellow seems to have retained a copy of this tape and is playing it at cocktail parties and the like here in New York City. If this is true, I am sure it is very amusing to the listeners but not very helpful to your image as a thoughtful and responsible newsman.

If the story is not true, please let me know and I will work out the details for a low-profile denial. If, on the other hand, it is true, please advise me and we will prepare a cover of sorts, perhaps passing it off as a youthful prank. In any event, let us see if we can't contact this Ernie Steinberg chap and straighten him out.

I can see no purpose in your discussing this matter with anyone else in the company. There is no point in feeding a vicious rumor.

Thank you for your cooperation.

Bill Farley
News Publicity

Holy cow, I said to myself. Also several other things. This could be worse than a paternity suit. There really *is* such a tape. But I made it years and years ago. Me and a guy named Ernie Steiner. It was a gag, to be played in a prop outhouse at a fraternity dance. I called my brother Bob. He knew about the tape. I asked him if he knew what the hell was going on. He laughed and confessed it was all a joke. He, Bill Farley and Steiner were friends. Practical joke.

Two can play that game. My producer, Art Browne, a short-haircut, West Point type whom I like anyway, checked with Primo to see if he'd ever talked to this guy Farley in publicity. Never, Primo said.

Sound of dialing. "Ahem. This is Al Primo," Art Browne says. Then he gave it to him. How come this letter hadn't been brought to his attention? What the hell did the publicity department think it was up to? Goddammit, Jim Bouton is under suspension as of now until this whole thing is investigated and ...

On the other end of the phone there was a hollow laugh. "Ha, ha. It was just a joke, Mr. Primo. Gee whiz, Mr. Primo, I wish you had checked with me first about it. Golly, this is terrible, Mr. Primo."

And the more he apologized, the more Art Browne laid it on. "Well, we can't afford anything like this, even if it was supposed to be a joke. A tape like that is a serious matter." And so on, until we both felt the kid was about to go out the window. Then we told him yes, it was indeed a joke. He was very grateful.

Try to practical-joke the practical joker, will he?

Now take humor. Somehow I'd always get into trouble around the clubhouse trying to do funny things. Like the time I tried to run for player representative on the Yankees. I wrote what I thought was a pretty funny flyer. No one laughed and I didn't get elected. I hardly even got any votes. You think I learned something from all of that? Nah. This is the note I put up on the bulletin board in the ABC newsroom:

Attention! As you know, I'm writing a book called "I'm Glad You Didn't Take It Personally" and I intend to have a chapter on the Eyewitness News team. If anyone has any anecdotes or stories to tell about any member of the Eyewitness News team, I'd be glad to include them in the book. It doesn't matter how obscure the stories are or how wild. I want to know about things like Roger Grimsby's sex life, if any; Al Primo's "problems"; degenerate film editors and similar stories. It doesn't matter if they're not true. The last time I included those kinds of stories in a book, no one got hurt and a good time was had by all. But if you don't send me any anecdotes I'm going to have to make them up myself and I'm sure you wouldn't want that.

Yours in sport,
Jim Bouton

I understand some people laughed. Others got nervous, and somebody tore the note off the board, wrinkled it up in a hot fist and threw it away. Then somebody else picked it up, smoothed it out and hung it back on the board, and I felt called upon to write on the bottom, "Hey, this is only a joke."

Also, beaver shooting. Now don't be alarmed, ladies. It's not true that Grimsby can look through the tube right into your bedroom, even though if you watch his eyes closely, you think he can. I'm talking about beaver shooting among the TV staff. The best shots we get are courtesy of John Schubeck, our bachelor. He's also our arts man, meaning he does theater and movie reviews, goes to museums, gallery openings, things like that. Possibly as a result, he comes by with some very solid chicks. I mean for the eleven o'clock news. They sort of sit around and wait for him to do his bit, then off they go to heaven knows what glories. Until they do, the rest of us do a lot of staring, especially when they happen to be bra-less and see-through. One night Grimsby's comment was "Anybody got an ice cube?"

Another thing that reminded me of baseball was that long walk to the studio. At ABC the newsroom is at one end of the block and the studio at the other. So you go outside for a brisk walk through the night air just before you go on. I remember my first trip, walking along with my script (yes, children, I do write my own stuff) folded neatly in my pocket, checking to see if it was there about every two seconds, perceiving everything sharply, as though for the first time. It was like coming in from the bullpen. The grass feels strange under your feet, the sounds of the crowd are sharp in your ear, even the odors are somehow more pungent. And as I walked toward the studio, the streetlamps seemed etched sharply against the sky, the concrete seemed as soft as grass under my feet—I felt as though I were floating. And under my Channel 7 blazer I could feel my heart pumping the way it used to when New York was written across my chest, or Houston.

There was a lot of fluster at the beginning, the way you are flustered when you are a rookie. The finger under the camera to give me my starting cue was a dagger. The script was my enemy. How much to look down, how much to look up, when to stop talking on the film cue, when to start. Well, I survived. Barely.

Not that I would want all those athletes out there to think it's really all that easy. It's hard, sometimes sweaty work. And what I could tell you about camera crews . . . But I won't. They have a very tough union. Besides, a light man once told me that he could make anybody he wanted to look like an Indian. So I'd better say here that the men in the crews are the nicest, sweetest, most put upon, most underpaid, most misunderstood, most talented men in America. Okay fellows?

Finally there is the problem of The Big Star. The Red Sox have Carl Yastrzemski. Washington has Denny McLain. Los Angeles has Richie Allen. ABC has Howard Cosell.

Understand this about Howard—he's good. He was, as far as I know, the first TV sports man to try to do a reporting job. He is the man who asked the tough question, who approached sports heroes with something less than slack-jawed admiration. Howard has mellowed in recent years, and he had rather a rough experience with Monday night pro football. But I'd still rather listen to Cosell's nasal, often overblown, commentary than the smooth, pointless, pandering and shilling of most TV sports people. I don't want to be like Cosell. For one thing, he doesn't approach things with enough humor. At the same time, I consider him a pioneer and, as such, entitled to a certain amount of respect.

Unfortunately, a lot of the people around Cosell don't look at things that way. They react to his personality here and now. And his personality is, well, abrasive.

QUESTION: "Where's Cosell?"

ANSWER: "He's out walking his pet rat."

Among the boys at ABC, Cosell is described

as looking like a lookout at a gang bang, and they tell delicious, probably apocryphal stories about him. There's the one about Floyd Patterson. Howard Cosell and a group of ABC radio news guys are sitting around talking about boxing. A dispute arises about a fact in the life of Patterson, then the heavyweight champion. "I'll call Floyd," Cosell says. The radio men are properly impressed. Sounds of dialing. "Hello, Floyd? This is Howard." Pause. "Howard, Floyd. HOWARD!" Pause. Smiles are breaking out on the faces of the radio guys. One of them giggles. Then, quietly, in an abashed voice, "Howard Cosell, Floyd."

Most of these stories are, of course, about Howard's basic insecurity, which he attempts to hide behind this enormous bluster. The bluster is more annoying than the insecurity.

So there's the one about the time Howard was called in to see Elton Rule, the new president of ABC. Cosell had no way of knowing whether it was going to be a pat on the back or a kick in the ass, so on the way to the meeting he was saying to the people in the car, "How long have you known me? A long time, right? Be honest with me. Do you know anybody better in the business? I'm a pro. Tell me, who's better? Who's as good?"

The meeting with the new president went well. Howard had been called in for a pat on the back. When he returned to his car he was his old self. "What the hell is this? I don't have to take this kind of crap. I'm a busy man. The president of ABC calls me in and wastes my time. I got a lot more important things to do. Let's go."

Of course television isn't exactly the kind of business that gives you a great sense of security. For example, Cosell has been moved—within the six o'clock news show—from six-thirty to six forty-five. The reason is that there was a drop of two or three points in the ratings at six-thirty, and the trick is to find out if Cosell has been turning people off. That's like a starting pitcher being sent to the bullpen to find out if he still has it.

I've got to give Howard points for toughness, though. Eyewitness News promotion has this thing that all the reporters are likable because they like each other. It really is a good crew and we do like each other (possibly because we don't have to go on two-week road trips). Anyway, in order to show how much we like each other we all sit through the entire news show and then, under the credits, we're shown talking to each other, putting our arms around each other, the whole *schmeer*. Not Howard, though. He shows up just before his bit, does it, and he's gone. And no one dares say anything to him about it. Except that when we're shown in ads, loving each other, Howard is never in the picture.

Despite this toughness, Cosell does seem rather over-sensitive about the possibility of competition. He swears to a lot of people that he was influential in bringing me to ABC. At the same time he'll bad-mouth me around town and to Al Primo and other ABC people, complaining of what a bad job I've been doing and how nobody likes me.

Example: It was reported in the spring of 1971 that Curt Blefary had shown up at the Yankee camp, twenty-five pounds lighter. "All water," Blefary was quoted as saying. "Melted ice cubes, no doubt," I suggested innocently in my little TV piece. Well, Cosell went wild. He didn't know what was wrong with the kid, he went around saying. The kid just didn't know what was going on. The kid just didn't have it. He buttonholed any number of ABC people and told them that Mike Burke, the president of the Yankees, had called him (Cosell) to complain. He said the whole Yankee organization was in a fury. He said Curt Blefary should sue.

It happened that shortly after all this Cosell sound and fury I was in Fort Lauderdale (with camera crew) and I asked around. Blefary wasn't angry, I found out. Not about the ice cubes. He just hated *Ball Four*. As for Mike Burke: "He called *me*. I'm not upset about the ice-cube line. I didn't even know what he was talking about. Why the hell would I call Howard Cosell?"

This wasn't the first time Cosell put words about me into Burke's mouth. When I was first hired by ABC he was around screaming that Burke was terribly upset. Wrong. I know because Bob Fishel, who runs the Yankee publicity department and is famous for telling the truth (an odd combination that), said, "Quite the contrary. Mike seemed happy about you getting the job."

Every once in a while I managed to get someone just the merest little bit angry at me, some player or coach, who as a result vows not to speak to me again as long as he lives. I do this, of course, professionally. In search for truth. And every time I did get somebody angry, Howard was sure to bring him on as an honored guest on his six o'clock show. That's supposed to show how well-liked Howard and his pet rat are.

Take Weeb Ewbank. Weeb's the famous coach of the New York Jets, a nice round little man who's hard to upset. I managed. I did a short interview with him and the last question I asked went like this: Weeb, coaches sometimes sell their players on the idea that in order to be successful they have to live a particular life style—no girls, plenty of sleep, discipline and short hair. Did you ever feel that way, and have you changed your mind since coaching Joe Namath?

Weeb got a funny look on his face, like he was someplace off in space. Well, he said, he could tell what a person was like just by looking at him. Like one time this guy came out for a job on the Jets and he had a beard and he wasn't hired because Weeb didn't think he looked right. After all, Weeb could tell a lot about a guy dressed like that and wearing a beard and on and on until he began to realize he was talking too much and saying some things that made him sound foolish. He didn't altogether stop talking, but his voice trailed off into a mumble. Thank you, Weeb Ewbank, I said. Then, as he walked away, he turned around and said, "You're never going to get anywhere asking questions like that."

I thought that was rather sweet of him. So I finished the piece by telling everybody out there just what Weeb had said. And I added, "When you're starting out like I am, you're grateful for any suggestions."

Just for that, Weeb doesn't talk to me anymore. Not only that, he's given orders that none of his Jet players are to come on the air with me. Well, I can live without the Jets and I suspect I'll be with ABC long after Ewbank is fired as Jet coach. But that's not the point. The point is that as soon as Howard Cosell got wind of my little problem, guess who his six o'clock guest was. Give that man a cigar, Weeb.

And one time friend Howard left a note on my desk that Bob Hope would be conducting a press conference on his golf tournament at 4 P.M. When I arrived with a camera crew all I found were crumbs on the table, dirty glasses and empty hors d'oeuvres trays. The conference had been scheduled for two o'clock.

Okay, anybody can make a mistake. Except I understand the same kind of thing used to happen to Lou Boda all the time.

The thing Howard Cosell probably doesn't understand about me is that I don't want his job. I don't want the six o'clock news. I don't want to be the biggest man in the industry. Right now, all I want is to learn to do the eleven o'clock news as well as I think I should be doing it. I want to spend a lot of time with my kids while they're growing up and still need me. No matter what Howard Cosell thinks, that's what I really want. And if I can't find that with ABC in New York, I'll be willing to try it with some other famous network in Seattle or Houston or Louisville. There might even be a job for me someplace in baseball. Don't laugh.

2

THE LAST
GREAT HALF SEASON
OF J. BOUTON

The spring was always my time of year, even when my arm was gone. That's because the pitchers are always ahead of the hitters in the spring, and I was always ahead of the rest of the pitchers. It wasn't difficult to get ahead. All I had to do was work harder than everybody else. I mean work until the pitching coach said, "Okay, Jim, you've had enough."

And then I said, "That's all right. I'll take a few more."

A few more pickups, a few more laps, a few more anything until I was so exhausted it would take me an hour just to unbutton the top button of my uniform. But it made a helluva nimpression, as they say. That and my tan. I always used the Whitey Ford formula on that, keeping my hat off and my face in the sun as much as possible. The tan makes you look two years younger and twice as fit.

And in the spring of 1970, a fairly eventful year in my life, I needed to make a nimpression.

I needed to more than anybody—well, almost anybody—knew. It wasn't only because at the age of thirty-one I had come to depend on a singularly unreliable knuckleball to get me past the increasingly formidable hitters in the National League. (The more I depended on my knuckleball, the more formidable they got.) It was because I had written *Ball Four*. You might have heard of it.

In February of 1970 almost nobody had. I reported to the Houston Astros camp in Cocoa, Florida, and went to work harder than anybody else. If I say so myself, I had a terrific spring. Big year, I thought, big year. If I got ten wins by the time the book comes out, everybody will say it's a helluva book. If we're on the way to a pennant, I'll sell a zillion. And if I pitch this way, they'll love me around here no matter what they think of the book. Can't miss, I told myself.

Of course I had some nagging doubts. Not about me and not about the Houston Astros. Hell, I once thought the Seattle Pilots could win the American League pennant. They couldn't even keep their American League franchise. I got optimism built into me like a robin with one end of a ten-foot earthworm in its beak. And I never doubted that *Ball Four* was a good book, a funny book and an honest book. (Somebody later on was to accuse me of being only 97 percent honest, and all I can say to that is that nobody's perfect.) But I did worry about how the book would be received—by baseball, by the club, by my teammates. It didn't take any super-brain to know that baseball and baseball players weren't used to 97 percent honesty, maybe not even 50 percent. As many people around baseball were to say, some things are better left unsaid. In baseball the phrase is, "He's a great guy. Wouldn't say shit if he had a mouthful." I believe this stems from a corner of the American mind which says: Don't talk about religion or politics, it will only get you into an argument. Don't offend. Don't get anybody angry. If you don't talk about it, it didn't happen. Well, I don't believe that. I believe that things are better said. If there are disagreements, okay, let's argue. Kicking things under the rug never did anything but lump up the rug. Besides, I knew there was a lot of fun in *Ball Four*, and I hoped the humor would be what everybody noticed most. That's what I hoped.

The spring was beautiful and I finished it in a great burst of glory. I beat the Yankees. Not only that, I drove in a run by faking a bunt and then driving the ball past the third baseman when he came charging in. It wasn't exactly like coming back to Yankee Stadium and beating them on their own turf, a pleasure I had promised myself the previous season but had never achieved, and it was only a spring game and it was in the Astrodome and I only went seven innings. But it was an all-around total, completely marvelous day. For two days—while the Yankees were beating us twice—I walked around with a grin on my face.

Looking back, I'm glad I was so happy. It was my last spring, and I'm one of the last of the big apes about baseball. I mean playing it and doing the idiot things with the guys in the clubhouse, in the bullpen and at the orgies. The game knocks me out.

Anyway, that big performance against the Yankees just about sewed up a starting spot for the knuckleball kid. And in my first start I beat Atlanta. I gave up five runs in the ninth, but Fred Gladding saved it for me. The point was, though, I had given up only four hits in the first eight innings and, would you believe, I got three hits myself. This so delighted a man from the Houston *Post*, Clark Nealon, that he wrote:

Our thrill of the season so far came out of Jim Bouton's total effort in his Saturday night performance which came close to being a classic. Jim's battle was an example of all out effort by a total athlete that we wish we could have showed every young player in town, as well as a lot of big leaguers. Here's a guy who is almost all the way back from a numbing arm injury, a picture of courage and hustle, fielding, hitting, going from first to third on singles to right, playing

44

the whole package for all it's worth. And it took the fans only a few innings to appreciate it with repeated ovations. This, gents, is what the true game is all about.

Gee, it was almost as good as seeing my picture on a bubble-gum card.

In spite of that game and a few other good ones, when I look back I'm convinced—in the front, or sane, part of my head—that I was finally sent to the minors because of my poor pitching and not because of the book. Harry Walker promised he'd judge me as a pitcher and not as an author. Unfortunately, he did. Still, every once in a while—in the back, or paranoid, part of my head—I wonder.

I lost the next game I pitched, one of your classic knockout jobs by the Giants. Even so, my knuckleball was really jumping around, because to that point I had only five walks and fourteen strikeouts, a much higher ratio than I had even when I was throwing hard. It was the third game that really broke my heart. We were playing the Pirates and were tied at 1–1 in the sixth. I'd given up only two hits. Richie Hebner was on first after walking. (I looked it up.) And Willie Stargell was coming up again.

Of course, we had talked about Stargell before the game. "Smoke him inside," I thought to myself. The consensus was that he was a good knuckleball hitter. I nodded. That's like sending a lion tamer into the cage without his chair and whip. Before the game began, Johnny Edwards, my catcher, reminded me that Stargell was a good knuckleball hitter. Then Stargell reminded me that he was a good knuckleball hitter. First time up he tagged one to the center fielder. I mean he drilled hell out of it, a bullet. So now, in the sixth, I got two strikes on him and a good memory. I also figure, hell, I'm in a tie game and if I walk him I'm moving the winning run to scoring position with Al Oliver, a good hitter, coming up next. So I decided to try to sneak a fastball over on him. And he decided to sneak it over the wall. A blast. It may still be moving. Over the whole wall in Forbes Field. I mean the roof too. The whole thing. The guys in the infield were snickering behind their gloves at the majesty of the blow.

I got out of the inning and into the dugout and Harry Walker said, "You can't throw a fastball to Stargell." Harry was right again. We lost, 3–1.

In my next game, against the Cubs, I got hurt. I was on second base (I'd become a hitting fool —over .300. Harry Walker had added at least 200 points to my batting average). Jimmy Wynn got a single and Salty Parker, the third-base coach, sent me in. He really had a lot of faith in the kid. The trouble was, I could see what was coming and I had time to think. This is very dangerous. I thought and thought and I decided I could score if I knocked the catcher down. J. C. Martin was his name. He's not a little guy. I could only knock him down if I took him by surprise. Jim Bouton trying to score from second on a single is a pretty good surprise as a starter. Unfortunately, I couldn't tiptoe. Martin heard me coming and got himself firmly planted just as I hit him. If I'd arrived a split second sooner, I'd have destroyed him. As it was, I was not only out, I jammed my left shoulder so bad I couldn't pitch for ten days. Norm Miller, my trusty roommate, had to help me on with my shoes and socks. (He's going to make somebody a good wife one of these days.) I believe that might have been a turning point, because those ten days of inactivity turned out to have a long-range effect on the knuckleball.

Couple of things about that play. It was good old-fashioned hardball, with a bit of Pete Rose coming out in me. If it had happened in an All-Star game or a World Series, I would have scooped up a lot of glory. As it was, all I got was Leo Durocher, the Cub manager, calling it a chickenshit play. Imagine that from old blood-and-guts. Also, the next time I came to bat against the Cubs, I got hit on the hand.

When I came back after my injury I was able to beat the Cubs 7–2, going all the way for my second win. First time up, Bill Hands, the Cub pitcher, knocked me on my ass. I was kind of flattered. I mean they *remembered*. "Hey, we all even now?" I yelled out to Hands. He didn't say anything, which was scary. I'd have hated to get into a head-hunting duel with my knuckleball. It's like being unarmed.

The nice thing about it all was that the ball nicked my left hand, I went down to first base, and wound up scoring a run. This touched off a rally and eventually Hands had to be taken out for a pinch hitter. It was his first loss, my second win. That's what you get for throwing at the old Bulldog. That's what you get for throwing at *anybody*. Take that, Leo Durocher.

By the time the season started there were a lot of rumors about the book. I caused them all. Look, I didn't know how much interest the book would stir up. I was a little nervous that it might not get noticed at all. Also I wanted to prepare people for when it came out. I wanted them to be ready for the kind of book it was. So at every opportunity I talked up the book to newspapermen.

Some of the lines I used:

I was going to write a book when I got famous. But I decided I couldn't wait any longer.

If the book was a movie, it would be rated X. (I borrowed that one from Shecter, the old rogue.)

Bill Freehan's diary will be Pablum next to *Ball Four*.

By the time my campaign was over, the head-line in a San Diego paper read: "ALL BASEBALL TREMBLING."

Well, me too. For a variety of reasons. One of them was the way I was pitching. I'd made five starts and you could say I'd done well enough in three of them, although I got only two wins. What the heck, it's no disgrace getting beat 3–1 by Pittsburgh. After I beat the Cubs I told Harry Walker he could use me in relief, too, if he wanted. He took me at my word. Foolish man. I pitched a couple of shutout innings and then the knuckle-ball seemed to go home to wherever knuckleballs go home to. Even Hoyt Wilhelm has the prob-lem. Except his knuckler must live close by and takes only short trips home. I think mine lived in Hong Kong. In almost no time at all my ERA had ballooned up over 6.00. Although I hate to do it, I believe I can blame part of it on the book.

After the first article came out in *Look*, I thought I could feel a difference in the atmos-phere around the club and around the ballpark. Where I used to get kind of a big hello from peo-ple along the dugout, people along the fence and people outside the park—policemen and ushers and autograph hounds—they suddenly seemed very reserved. Some of them didn't say anything, not even hello. And the players, I thought, weren't as quick to come over to my locker and goof around. Fred Gladding always came over and laid some Crazy Guggenheim on me, so I would do it back to him, and he didn't come around for days. I thought I could see a wall building up and I decided I would put a letter up on the bulletin board explaining why I wrote the book and what I felt should be the sane reaction to it and why I didn't want it to affect our relationship. Then I decided against it. Although it may not seem like it, baseball players are like people. They enjoy the legends and the myths they've grown up with and they don't like to see them blurred.

When I was with Seattle I was working daily on the diary. I was also spending a lot of my free time thinking about the knuckleball, just walking around with a ball in my hand. I'd even hold one when I was driving to and from the park. I knew I had to have the knuckleball—a good one—if I was going to hang on long enough to write the damn book. At the start of this season, though, I figured I had it down. I could start just where I had left off. I was encouraged in the spring and by the first few games I pitched. I guess I really had dropped back, though, because when the knuckler went, it was gone. I was helpless. Besides, I didn't have any spare time to think about it. The shit hit the fan when the excerpts began running in *Look* in May and I was besieged all the time. Reporters, television, the phone never stopped ringing. There were stories in every paper in every town for days on end. Most of them were hostile beyond belief. I was delighted that the book was getting so much attention, but I was tense and nervous, too. I found it difficult to sleep. It was tremendously exciting, great fun —and hell on the knuckleball.

There were other pressures. Like Harry Walker calling a meeting.

You have to understand about Harry. I think he's a good manager. He knows the game. And guys play for him. If they don't, he calls them in for a conference. It's better to play for him.

I don't mean he's a Vince Lombardi and can chew you into a quivering wreck, making you certain you are lower than whale shit. Harry gives you fifty minutes on The War, or half an hour on Civil Rights, twenty minutes on The Family, maybe an hour on The Flag.

He'll even give it to everybody in general on the bus. He sees ballplayers giving each other the slap handshake (instead of the firm grip and steely eye) and he says, "Now *that's* what's wrong with the world today." The bus goes by a bunch of long-hairs and Harry says, "Now *that's* what's wrong with the world today." It gets to you. I remember one time with two out I struck out the third hitter on a knuckleball that got by the catcher and wound up giving up three runs.

Know what I said to myself? "Now *that's* what's wrong with the world today."

Harry's army talk was the most puzzling. It was always about how the army was a big outfit and, sure, they made mistakes, but everybody makes mistakes, even baseball, and you have to handle a whole lot of people and people don't understand what that's like.

I'm not certain where General Patton fits in there, but it's someplace. Like President Nixon, Harry never should have seen that movie. He got it all mixed up with reality. We'd get going bad and Harry would come up with Patton, how he didn't have time to fool with details, how he *acted*. That's why he (Patton) had to get up there and throw the cart off the bridge. He had to get the troops through. He couldn't bother about this guy or that guy, or the driver; he had to get an army moving. And we had to take Patton's values and apply them to ourselves. That way lay victory.

Civil Rights: Look at every neighborhood they move into. Starts to go downhill right away. They just tear things down. You try to teach them things and you can't do it. You try to hire them and they won't work. They're not all bad, of course. There are some who are good and want to work. But most of them, you can't do anything for them.

The Family: The family is the most important thing. After all, this is just a job and it's fun, but you got to go back to your family. If you have a crisis, your family sticks together and you keep all your problems to yourself, because you know you have to be united.

The Flag: The flag is important because it's a symbol of what this country stands for and all the men who died. The people who damage the flag, or wear it for pants, don't understand the guys who died for us. It's a symbol of this country and that's what wrong with the world today.

The trouble is, I think, that Harry's world stopped, the way you can stop a motion picture projector, the day the big war ended. Harry tries to adjust, but he can't. His values are largely decent—and twenty-five years old. Perhaps that's why Dick Young wrote a column last summer extolling Harry as one of the sages of modern America. Harry Walker and Dick Young think a lot alike.

I believe at least some of that column deserves being preserved between hard covers. The lead, for example:

This business of a handslap after a homer instead of a man's heartfelt handshake. Harry Walker doesn't go for it, but Harry Walker is 52, like me, and not to be trusted.

"If a handshake means anything, then do it right," says Harry Walker. "Don't give it a brush. It's typical of the careless way things are done today."

And this:

. . . He [Walker] said a writer came to him in Philly the other day and was talking about their new stadium. "I asked him what the name of it was, and he said Veterans Stadium, but there was some objection to it, and there was talk of another name. I asked him why, and he said because people are fed up with war and war memorials.

"Imagine that, Philadelphia, of all places. Right there where this country started, trying to do right by honoring the veterans and some people raising a fuss about it. The idea of naming a stadium like that for the veterans is to make the people who have so much here, the liberty and the freedom to express themselves, let them know where it all came from. Let them remember the men who died to give it to them.

"Nobody wants war. Hell, I gave 2½ years to it, but how do you walk away from it? I made a talk the other day to the Rotary Club. I told them baseball is like the United States. It's not perfect. There are some things wrong with it, for sure, but it's the best thing around. Everybody else in the world would like to have what this nation has, and most everybody would like to have what these ballplayers have."

Anyway, two days before the first installment of *Ball Four* was due out in *Look,* but well after advance copies had circulated, Harry called a meeting. It was the first real rumble.

In many ways it was a typical clubhouse meeting. Harry talked, and the players tried to keep from laughing. Even me. And I should have been crying. Because the meeting, it soon became apparent, was about me.

"Now this is important," Harry Walker said. "This is right from the Commissioner and it's important. What the Commissioner says is this: he doesn't want to read or hear about anyone knocking his fellow teammates or the people who run the game. The Commissioner doesn't want us saying or doing anything that would in any way reflect badly on baseball and he says he's serious about this. He says he's going to crack down on anyone who does it and he's going to crack down with fines or by suspension from baseball. He absolutely will not have anyone doing this."

I couldn't help it. I had to put my arm over my face, and I peeked out at the other guys and they were all looking at me and trying not to giggle. They were trying not even to smile. Harry doesn't like smiles and he's always looking around the room for them. My roomie, Norm Miller, made mouth motions at me from across the room. "You're through," he said. "You're through." He looked very happy about it.

After Harry was through with his speech, he looked around the room and decided to give it again. It was almost exactly the same thing, except for the ending. This time, when he wound up, he pointed a long finger directly at me and said, "And that goes for you." He paused for a moment, as though realizing he was being too specific, and added, "And any of you other guys." But he wasn't looking at the other guys, he was looking at me.

Let me explain about the little tickle of fright under the giggle. At this stage I never thought of myself as anything but a pitcher. Pitching is what I knew, and the game is what I loved. Writing *Ball Four* was fun. I never intended it to end my career. A few weeks before, in fact, I'd asked Jim Owens, our pitching coach, one-time swinging member of the Philadelphia Phillies' Dalton Gang and, by extrapolation, a guy I figured knew the score, "Hey, they nervous in the front office about this book?"

"Probably," Owens said.

"What do you think will happen if they get upset about some of the things in it?"

"Dunno," Jim Owens said. "Depends on how you're doing at the time."

That's the way things go in baseball. You could be North American dum-dum one and if your batting average is over .300, people listen to you like you were Secretary of State. On the other hand, you could be a reasonable, intelligent, well-informed, educated, handsome righthanded pitcher with a record of 2–3 and they'd say, "What the hell does he know?"

When Eddie Kranepool of the Mets called Carl Yastrzemski a yo-yo (this was when Yaz was trying to break the players' strike), a lot of people jumped on him. They didn't argue that Yastrzemski *wasn't* a yo-yo, just that Kranepool wasn't a good enough player to say it. Translation: You have to be a Frank Howard to call Yastrzemski a yo-yo, or you have to be having a hot month or a hot week. You're only as smart as your ERA.

Essentially, then, it didn't really matter what I said in the book. If I was a winning pitcher I could be Jack the Ripper in my spare time and people would pat me on the head. Except I didn't think this was my year to win twenty games. So when Harry started pointing a finger at me, I laughed, but I got a funny feeling down the back of my neck just the same.

And my roommate wasn't any help. After the meeting he came over, stuck out his hand and said, "Good-by Jim. It's been nice knowing you."

Then Tommy Davis came over and said, "Tomorrow, Jim, when you come to the ball park, there won't be anything in your locker." He put his hand on my shoulder and his eyes were serious and sad. "You know that, don't you?"

Of course he was kidding. But crazy thoughts do go through your mind. Suppose, I thought, this was the year the Astros could win the pennant.

Suppose when the book comes out they get all upset about the stuff I said about them. Suppose this ruins our chances. Suppose we lose nine out of ten. Suppose it's not too late to knock out the whole last part of the book and end it at the point when I got traded from Seattle. Well, I went out and ran a couple of laps around the field and slowly my sanity returned. I said to myself, listen, they'll read the book—everybody in baseball will read the book—and they'll have a good laugh. Maybe they'll make a few policy changes to correct the evils I discussed (in recognition of my insightful brilliance) and accept the book as mature adults should. I thought that. I really did.

Meanwhile, the Astros weren't doing any better than I. We lost seven of eight on the road, and the happiness of the spring was giving way to the grumpiness of reality. I've often been asked why I think the Astros always do so poorly on the road. One theory is that the team was put together just to play in the Astrodome. Another is that we knew how to play the air conditioning. My own theory is that we lost on the road because of the curfew.

The players had their own theories about why we were losing. Mickey Mouse. One picayune thing after the other was put on us until we were drowning in a sea of cotton batting.

There was, for example, the Exergenie. This

was a contraption we were supposed to use every day to build up everything including our eyeballs. Well, some of the guys weren't doing the Exergenie. And some of them were and were forgetting to sign up. So after a loss one day, the word came down. If you don't sign up for the Exergenie, you'll get fined. So everybody signed up. But it was like before. There may have been a lot of signing; there just was not very much doing.

About a week later it was the weigh-ins. If you forgot to weigh in before getting dressed, you had to take your clothes off and start all over. It was a pain in the neck. That's what they wanted.

The next edict was that there would be no card playing in the back room of the clubhouse. Then there would be no flip games. (The ball is batted gently to a line of players who flip it back and forth until the ball touches the ground. It's a good game, passes the time, and probably adds to your manual dexterity. Nothing wrong with it, except we were losing.) The rationale was that instead of playing cards or the flip game we should be concentrating on the game, the game, the game.

Then we had extra workouts. Then they started cracking down on curfew. Then they began to keep written records of wind sprints. Mel McGaha was in charge of counting them, and one day Joe Pepitone didn't do his five wind sprints and he got called into the office and they fined him, and there was hell to pay for days. Then, because the pitchers weren't going nine innings, they took us all over to the old Colt stadium and made us run a mile. They compared our times with those we ran in spring training. Fortunately we were all at least thirty seconds better. Heaven knows what would have happened if we weren't. Guillotine, probably.

Then golf was banned. (Swimming was always against the rules, possibly on the grounds that a tan was bad for you.) The golf ban did no good so it was decided the coaches shouldn't play golf either. (And why not? Doesn't playing golf make you stupid? Or is it the other way around?) Then it was ruled that *everybody* had to have a roommate. (And Jim Owens said, "You think *you've* got it bad. I've got to room with a *coach*.") Then we lost a game in Philadelphia and food was banned and the curfew went from two and a half hours after the game to two hours.

Then Harry set a workout for an off day in Philadelphia which happened to conflict with an appointment I'd made with a local television station. I was in a cab with Bob Watson and Mike Marshall and I wondered out loud if I should ask for permission to miss the workout and Watson said definitely not, unless I liked to watch Harry blow his stack and Mike Marshall said hell, you know how unimportant the workout is and this is a commitment you made a long time ago. So I asked Harry and it turned out Watson was right. Harry blew his stack.

I called the lady at the television station to tell her the sad story and she burst into tears. She said she had made all the arrangements and studio time is very expensive and she would now lose her job, probably. So she called the head of the station and he called the Phillies' public relations man who called Harry who blew his stack again. Then the girl called him and I called him and pretty soon he was up to his ears telling people no and finally he said to me, "You, you're one of the reasons this team is losing, you and your book. You don't have your mind on the game and the guys don't have their minds on the game. If they did, they'd be playing better ball." One of the reasons Harry was so upset was that before I called about getting out of the workout Joe Pepitone had asked permission to miss the workout in order to go to New York and handle some legal difficulties with his wife. Harry said okay. Then I called. It must have seemed like rats deserting a sinking ship.

The television thing was finally ironed out with no suicides by shifting the taping to late afternoon. I still don't know what wounds were left in Harry Walker's gentle heart.

At any rate, later in the season, when I distributed copies of *Ball Four* around the club, Harry's basic good nature had been restored. I had run up a couple of flights of steps to Harry's hotel room and I was puffing a bit when I got there. "You out of shape?" Harry said gently. He could be funny intentionally.

We sat down and talked for a moment, and Harry said, ah, he knew the club wasn't losing because of the book. He said he was so ill-tempered because we weren't winning. It was an apology.

That's another reason I'm so fond of Harry.

In the flyleaf of the book I gave him I wrote, "I have more respect and admiration for you than any manager I've ever played for." I meant it. I still do.

On May 24 I got a start against the Cincinnati Reds and was blasted out in the first inning. When a knuckleball doesn't knuckle it's not a knuckleball, it's a piece of cake, pound cake. I faced five hitters. Three of them got hits. One walked. I got only one out. The whole Cincinnati team was up in front of the dugout screaming at me. (Pete Rose and Johnny Bench seemed to be the loudest.)

"Shakespeare, you no-good rat-fink. Put that in your fucking book."

"Go write a book about *that*, rag arm."

And with the count ball three, "What's the title of your book?"

Let's see if I can explain what that did for my pitching. Looking back, I can only think I was overconcentrating. Super-overconcentrating. I'm

going to really do good here. Put everything I
got into it. Really throw the son of a bitch. Then
I'd miss and try even harder on the next one.
You can't pitch that way. Especially with a
knuckleball. Sometimes, with the fastball, you
get to throw nervous hard, harder and harder
the madder or more nervous you get. But the
knuckleball—half of it was in the head. And *all*
my head was in the dugout.

That wasn't the worst of it. The worst of it
was in New York. I'd been called for a meeting
with the Baseball Commissioner, fellow named
Bowie Kuhn. Although it was supposed to be a
secret meeting, somehow word got out. I mean
Dick Young guessed in print (or maybe he'd
been tipped off) I'd be called in, and so I felt
free to spread the word. Figured it couldn't do
the book any harm.

Spec Richardson, the Houston general manager, had told me that the Commissioner wanted
to have a talk with me when the team was in
New York ten days later. I called the Commissioner's office and spoke to his man Charley
Segar. I told him I'd be a lot happier if I could
hop on a plane and get it over with right away
rather than have it hang over my head for ten
days. But he said no, that wouldn't be necessary.
Not for him. For me, it was hell. I'd wake up in
the morning and as soon as I was conscious, my
stomach would churn over. I felt like, I don't
know, maybe like I'd killed somebody in an auto-

mobile accident or something, sort of helpless and terrible. I *knew* I hadn't done a bad thing, but I was afraid no one would ever see my side of it, never understand what I was trying to do.

In order to comfort me, Tom Griffin, pitcher, said that he knew what would happen when we got to New York. He said the Yankees would be waiting for me at the hotel and there would be a duel at high noon. Our bus would be driven from the airport along deserted streets; an occasional woman or child would be seen scurrying for shelter. We'd go into the hotel and the clerk would be hiding behind the desk, pointing to my key ten feet away. People would be concealed behind potted plants, ducking behind furniture.

Grif said he'd stick with me. Doug Rader volunteered to be a bodyguard. Jack DiLauro said he'd be my second and Norm Miller, my faithful companion, offered to keep his eyes on the door.

My wife said it was like living with a famous criminal wanted by the FBI.

When we finally got to New York, Dick Young was the guy with the shotgun. I wish it had been the FBI. Calling me a social leper was almost the least of it. The most of it was saying that because of the book the club was being torn by dissension. It wasn't true, but Young hoped it was and sometimes by saying things like that, you make them happen. Dick Young says we're torn by dissension. Hey, we are. So *that's* why we're losing so much. The truth was, of course, that we were a lot more torn by dissension when we played the good clubs than when we played the bad ones.

We were going from the hotel to Shea Stadium on Sunday, the day before my meeting with the Commissioner, when Jim Beauchamp, utility outfielder, hollered from the back of the bus, "Jim, when you go to see the Commissioner, don't worry about a thing. We're behind you seven percent."

That made me feel a lot better. Unfortunately, there was a baseball game too.

It was the first game of a doubleheader. You could tell things weren't going well for us, because I was warming up. I was worrried—about the crowd, I mean. This was home territory. My mother and father and my brothers and friends and relatives were in the stands. And I wondered how the fans would react. I tried to concentrate on the knuckleball and not think about the book. That's like saying to yourself, for the next two minutes don't think about elephants. The more I tried not to think about the book, I thought about the book, the book, the book.

The ball park was jammed, and as soon as I stuck my nose out of the bullpen in left field, the boos started. They washed over me like a flood of garbage. Nothing like it had ever happened to me before. (Omigod, what will Mom think?) I'd always had a sort of rapport with fans and if there had been any boos, they were scattered.

This was, well, it was like walking into a wall, nose first. It's because I'm an ex-Yankee, I told myself. It's because I'm in Dick Young country. It can't be because of the book, the book, the book. There's no book yet, only a couple of magazine articles. You know something? I don't even remember if I rode in from the bullpen or walked.

As I took my warmup pitches on the mound I was thinking, "Not bad, not bad. The knuckleball is going to be all right. You'll make out." Wrong again.

I was jocked. All I can remember is that I kept falling behind on the hitters. They were taking on me and I thought, the bastards, why the hell don't they swing? I walked a guy, gave up a hit, probably two, got somebody out, then another hit and here came Harry Walker.

"I got to get you out of here," he said.

"You're right, Harry," I said.

I walked off the mound and now that I was a loser, the booing was even worse. I wanted to do two things. I wanted to get away as fast as I could. And I wanted to stop and wave my fist at them and scream, you sons of bitches, if this was 1963 you wouldn't be booing your shitty heads off. What I did, of course, was get away as fast as I could. And I rooted against the Mets for the rest of the season.

All during the second game, for the first time

in my life, I prayed that I wouldn't get into it. For the first time, I knew I wouldn't do well. And I'll tell you, I didn't want to go up against that booing again.

I was supposed to have dinner with my folks after the game but I just didn't want to. I saw them outside the park and my Mom kissed me and told me to hang in there. They really felt bad. Not for themselves, for me. It was a tough day.

When I got back to the hotel there was a message to call Shecter and he asked me if I'd had dinner. I could've kissed him. We went to an Italian restaurant in the Village and a few drinks didn't hurt. After dinner we went over to the Lion's Head to have a few more drinks and on the way we picked up *The New York Times*. Bob Lipsyte had a column on the *Look* excerpts.

If the excerpts in *Look* are indicative of the book's content and style, Bouton should be given baseball's most valuable salesman of the year award. His anecdotes and insights are enlightening, hilarious and, most important, unavailable elsewhere. They breathe a new life into a game choked by pontificating statisticians, image-conscious officials and scared ballplayers.

Somebody out there understood. I had a lump in my throat when I finished reading it. There were other columns later, other good reviews from serious critics. None ever moved me more. And none, of course, could ever have come at so propitious a time.

I went back to the hotel, called Bobbie and read the column to her. Then I told her about Dick Young quoting Joe Pepitone as calling me "the horniest bleep in baseball." Presumably this meant that I went about in an advanced state of enraged sexuality from which no waitress, stewardess or passing grandmother was safe. I told her there were going to be a lot of personal attacks like that and there was nothing we could do about them. And she said, "That's all right, honey, I understand. Besides, you really are kind of horny."

It was the worst of days, and the best.

After that, everything got better, even my pitching. My ERA climbed steadily down from a peak of over 7.0. Even my old fastball put in an appearance. In a game against Atlanta, for instance, I came in with the bases loaded and had to face Hank Aaron and Rico Carty. I got Aaron to pop up a fastball and struck out Carty on five straight hard ones. You don't do that unless you're really pumping. Even so, there were only two other pitchers on the club with ERAs worse than mine. So on July 31, when I had a record of four wins and six losses and an ERA of 5.42, Harry Walker called me in and said he was sending me down to Oklahoma City. "It's not because of the book," Harry said.

I believed him. I really did. Except every once in a while the back of my head, the paranoid part, clicks in and I start wondering again.

3.

THE KING AND I

I acknowledge a deep debt to Bowie Kuhn, our Commissioner. There are some who say it's a quarter of a million. I consider that an exaggeration.

The reason for this debt is that he called me into his office to chat about *Ball Four*. As a result, there were headlines on every front page in the country. That's fame, and fame in the book business is fortune. If Bowie Kuhn and his public relations assistant, Joe Reichler, had entered into a conspiracy to sell copies of the book, they would have done nothing different. To this day a lot of people ask me what I paid the Commissioner. This is a base canard and I resent it. Kuhn is an honorable man and I could not have bribed him to do the marvelous things he did for me. I can only assume that he did them out of friendship.

Indeed, I have told him that more than once. One time was at the Baseball Writers' Dinner in Washington in January of 1971. I'd been asked to present an award to Jim Perry of the Minnesota Twins. When I got to the lectern I acknowledged the presence of the famous people on the dais, among them "Mrs. Mitchell, the wife of what'sizname, and Bowie Kuhn—and we all know what *he's* done for me." For some reason, my friend Bowie Kuhn just sat there, staring straight ahead, purple rising up his neck.

The Commissioner wanted no publicity about our meeting. So no one showed up but the Commissioner, his aides, Marvin Miller, head of the Major League Players Association; the Association attorney, Dick Moss; the AP, UPI, Reuters, *The New York Times, Daily News, Post,* Jerome Holtzman of the Chicago *Sun-Times,* assorted television crews and two hippies named Richard Feuer and Steve Bergen, carrying placards that read: "Jim Bouton Must Not Be Repressed" and "Bouton Is a Real Hero" and "No Punishment for Exposing the Truth" and "Kuhn: Stop Repression and Harassment." I flashed the kids the peace sign and smiled at everybody else.

We cooled our heels for about a half hour before the Commissioner met with us. We assumed he was busy with something else important. He couldn't have been angry or anything. Bowie Kuhn is famous for not getting angry or anything.

In fact, the first thing he said to us was that he didn't mean this meeting to become public.

Because it should be very obvious to everybody, he said, that the last thing he wanted to do was promote the sale of *Look* magazine or the book. I wonder what he meant by that.

I had made up my mind that I would not take a defensive position. The best defense in this situation, it seemed to me, was a good offense. Charge! "Wait a minute, Commissioner. I'd like you to know that I did not announce to the press that this meeting was taking place."

Of course. I'd been warned *not* to announce it. Do I look stupid? Never mind. Don't answer that.

"But I picked up a newspaper and Dick Young had it in his column that you would be calling me into your office. He didn't say might. He said will. I figured that since he's close to the baseball establishment it meant that he had been told. And once he wrote about it, I felt it was a matter of public knowledge. I couldn't really deny it when I was asked if I had been called in."

COMMISSIONER: Grumble, grumble, grumble.

Then, talking very earnestly, Bowie Kuhn, a graduate of Princeton, for fourteen years National League legal counsel, made three points. The first one was that he was very disappointed in me, Jim Bouton. He had known me to be a very cooperative person, that I had volunteered to go to hospitals and whatnot. (I always enjoyed going to whatnots.) So he couldn't understand what had come over me.

I might have protested that I was still the same

old Jim Bouton—cooperative, gentle and kind to my wife and children. Like I said, I had made up my mind to hang tough with the man. I wasn't going to grovel. I wasn't going to apologize. But Marvin Miller had suggested I say as little as possible. He wanted to let poor Bowie paint himself into a corner, hang himself with his own words, hoist himself on his own petard, give himself enough rope. So I just sort of tried to look friendly and open, like a big dog.

The Commissioner's second point was that he was shocked and disappointed and disgusted at what he had read in *Look*. (He quickly admitted he hadn't read the book, just the first of two excerpts in the magazine.) He said the excerpts in the magazine were so bad, he had to remove them from his home. He did not want his son to read them. He said, thirdly, that this was very bad for baseball and what did I have to say for myself?

I felt unleashed. "Well, I think you're wrong," I said. (I wanted to say, "I think you're full of shit." But what would the Commissioner's son have said?) "I can't imagine any kid over twelve not being able to read this book without embarrassment. They all know the words. And there aren't any words in the book that don't appear in a lot of modern writing and magazines. I think it gives an accurate view of what baseball and baseball players are like. As a result, I think people will be more interested in baseball, not less.

I think people are turned off by the phony goody-goody image. So I think you're wrong about what's good or bad for baseball."

He didn't like that much.

"I'll decide what's good and what's bad for baseball," he said. "That's my job, not your job."

"I suppose so. But I'm not obligated to write a book that only has good things about baseball in it."

"Well, you make your living in baseball, and you should support it. You owe it to the game because it gave you what you have."

"I always gave baseball everything I had. Besides, baseball didn't *give* me anything. I *earned* it."

COMMISSIONER: Grumble, grumble, grumble.

Then he said he wanted to be more specific. What he really meant was that he didn't believe the things I had written. So he began to go over them one by one.

"How widespread is the use of greenies? Who takes them?"

"It's all there in the book. Don Mincher says half the guys in the big leagues take them. I have no reason to doubt him. I know from personal knowledge that a lot of players take greenies. And I've taken greenies."

"What do they do for you?"

"Not much. Like I say in the book, they make you think you're doing better than you're actually doing."

COMMISSIONER: Grumble, grumble, grumble.

I should say here that I never said greenies were bad for you (or very good). I merely said in the book that people take them. This was widely denied, of course, but now the Commissioner has a committee of team physicians studying the problem. How can there be a problem that doesn't exist?

The Commissioner went on to another point. "Now you've got a part there that I think is going to be very bad for players' relationships with their wives and their marriages. You have Gary Bell telling Ray Oyler to bring home his socks because he left them under Oyler's bed. People are going to read that and they're going to think that ballplayers are sleeping with each other's wives."

Good grief, I thought, the man can't read. "Bowie, it was very clear that this was a joke. I said that the players have a *verbal* sexual liberation. And what they do is kid about it."

And he said, "You don't think people will really believe that it's just verbal, just a joke, do you?"

Well, in fact that's exactly what I thought. I thought it, because I meant it. Hell, players aren't screwing around with each other's wives. At least not as far as I know.

It turned out that maybe the Commissioner knew more about it than I did. At least later on somebody whispered into my shell-pink ear that there was a club (I won't name it, because I don't know for certain that the story is true) on which there was real trouble of exactly that sort. As an added attraction, there were supposed to be some ugly racial overtones. Anyway, a lot of trades were made and the problem was more or less overcome. The point is, though, that the Commissioner was supposedly aware of the problem and when he read the *Look* excerpt he thought I was trying to spill some hot beans. I plead innocent. Besides, if players were actually fooling around with each other's wives, I don't think we'd kid about it in the clubhouse. On the other hand, maybe we would.

The other big thing the Commissioner seemed concerned about was the kissing game the lads on the Seattle team played for a while. The idea was to sneak up to some hairy guy and kiss him —on the lips. It seemed rather fun at the time. I mean fun because it was disconcerting. All the guys were straight. They were. They were. They were.

KUHN: "It wasn't a good idea for you to make up a story like that. People are going to believe that the players actually kissed each other."

ME: "But they *did* kiss each other."

KUHN (incredulous): "On the *lips?*"

ME: "Full on the lips, Commissioner."

COMMISSIONER: Grumble, grumble, grumble.

I confess that I have foreshortened our actual conversation. The reason is that there was a lot of rambling. The Commissioner is a very deliberate speaker and has a tendency, besides, to repeat himself. And we seemed to argue after almost every sentence about whether this or that was good or bad for baseball or in between.

Then there was a lot of wrangling between the Commissioner and Marvin Miller. Part of the reason was that Miller wasn't going to let the Commissioner get away with anything. As he explained to me later, he had in mind Denny McLain walking into an informal meeting with the Commissioner and coming out with a half-season suspension. That's like the guy who walks into an informal talk with the DA and comes out in handcuffs, arrested and virtually convicted on his own testimony.

So when the Commissioner said he was not going to take any action "at this time," and that he wanted me to take this as a "warning," Miller jumped in fast.

"A warning against what, Bowie?" Miller said.

The Commissioner looked blank.

"Is this a warning against writing?" Miller said in that quiet way of his. "Is it a warning against writing about baseball? Is it a warning against using four-letter words?"

COMMISSIONER: Grumble, grumble, grumble.

Kuhn also said he couldn't get specific, that we all understood what he was talking about.

"No, I don't understand," Miller said. "I don't understand what you're talking about. You can't

subject someone to future penalties on such
vague criteria. Why, that's like a policeman
walking up to someone in a crowd and saying,
'I'm warning you.' Against what? The expression
on my face?"

COMMISSIONER: Grumble, grumble, grumble.

This discussion took about twenty minutes.
The rest of the two and a half hours were spent
discussing what to tell the press, or rather what
not to tell the press.

It was the Commissioner's first idea to have
no statement at all. But it was brought to his attention that there were too many press people
outside (not to mention the hippies) to get away
with anything like that. So he said, grumble, grumble, grumble, that, well, all right, *he* would issue
a statement and that I should not. "I'm asking
you not to issue a statement," is the way he put
it.

"Now wait a minute," Miller said. "You can't
ask him not to make a statement. If you're going
to make a statement, he has the right to make
one too."

This argument went on for a while and finally
I was asked to leave the room while Miller and
Moss stayed to talk about an appropriate way to
end the meeting which, I suspect, the Commissioner was now sorry he had called. I sat in an
adjoining office and Charley Segar, formerly of
the New York *Daily Mirror*, who was one of the
Commissioner's assistants before his recent re-

tirement, sat down and sort of looked at me. I looked back. I guess he felt he had to entertain me or something, because finally he said, "The league looks pretty balanced this year, doesn't it?" I nearly fell off my chair.

It was a scene right out of Pinter. There we sat, my doom being discussed in the next room (every once in a while I could hear voices raised into shouts) and we're talking about the *pennant race*. In June. Absolutely weird.

Segar and I went on this way for about forty-five minutes. Of course I was later able to reconstruct what went on in my absence. One thing was a marvelous bit of defense by Miller. When the Commissioner started talking about what was good for baseball, Miller interrupted with his own theory. He said something like this: "What you're saying is that what was good about the past was that the public had this image of the player wearing a halo. But I believe fans today are different. They're a lot more sophisticated and a lot more concerned with players as human beings. I could well make a case that something which took away this phony, unrealistic view of the life of a professional player and showed that it was a great deal more down to earth could be very good for baseball.

"You know, this simon-pure image is really not in the history of baseball. It only developed in relatively modern times. I can remember when I was a kid, I knew Babe Ruth was a woman chaser and a beer drinker and a lot of other things and this didn't turn me off Babe Ruth and baseball. I can remember reading one story after another of Grover Cleveland Alexander sipping bourbon in the bullpen and barely being able to walk to the mound and going out there and striking out the side. That was dramatic and made him all the more a romantic character."

The Commissioner said that wasn't his idea of baseball. Grumble, grumble, grumble.

Then there was the construction of the Commissioner's press release. The way it was, the Commissioner would write one, read it out loud, and Miller or Moss would say, no, that won't do. In one draft of a release, for example, the Commissioner said he "would not take any action at this time."

Miller pointed out that this would pose more questions than it answered. "The implication is that you're withholding any action for the time being, but may take action later," Miller said. "Is that what you mean?"

No, he didn't mean that. Grumble, grumble, grumble. And he'd write another release.

Finally this one was settled on:

"I advised Mr. Bouton of my displeasure with these writings and have warned him against future writings of this character. Under all the circumstances, I have concluded that no other action was necessary."

Miller wasn't very happy with that, either. He

particularly objected to "future writings of this character." He said he didn't know what it meant. At the same time, he had absolutely no control over what the Commissioner told the press. So he settled. The newspapers interpreted the statement as a slap on the wrist. In fact, it was nothing of the kind. In fact, it was nothing.

I've thought many times about why Kuhn brought me in altogether. It couldn't have been to get off that particular statement. I think there were certain pressures brought to bear upon him, perhaps by local newspapermen, perhaps by his public relations assistant; people saying, "Commissioner, you can't let him get away with that." I think the Commissioner believed, or was told to believe, that it would be an easy process. I'd come in, repent, say I was sorry I wrote the book, say the devil made me do it (actually everyone would have been delighted if I just blamed it all on Shecter) and leave repentant. I could tell he was surprised that I came in there hanging tough. And later on, I heard him say a couple of times on television that well, Jim was sorry about it all and everybody is entitled to make a mistake. What upset him most was that I wouldn't admit that *Ball Four* was one of mine.

After forty-five minutes with Charley Segar, I'd had enough. I knocked on the office door, stuck my head in and asked what the devil was going on. They invited me back in and at that point the discussion was about what *I* would say to the press. "I prefer that you not comment on what went on at this meeting," the Commissioner said.

And Miller said, "You can ask him not to comment on what went on at the meeting, but you can't ask him to say he accepts your view of things. He's got to be able to explain how he feels."

"Right," I said, feeling tougher than ever. You can tell when you've got somebody on the run. He says, grumble, grumble, grumble. "Commissioner, they're going to ask me whether I agree with your decision and I'm going to say I think I'm entitled to write a book."

COMMISSIONER: Grumble, grumble, grumble.

I know what he wanted. He wanted his little press release to go out and then he wanted us all to disappear. It's called arrogance.

What we agreed on, finally, was that I would not talk about what happened at the meeting. I'd say no comment. I could see why the Commissioner would want that. No one would believe what happened if I told anyway. But I could, it was agreed, talk about anything else I wanted to. So I went out into the Commissioner's front parlor and did my thing for television. I wouldn't want anybody to think I hated it. I've been told I have a little bit of ham in me. I'm surprised anybody noticed. I've tried to keep it secret. Anyway, I quote from the Associated Press dispatch:

Was he sorry about "Ball Four?"

"Absolutely not. I'm glad I wrote the book."

Wouldn't this publicity help the sales?

"That would be nice."

What did he think about the demonstration?

"Terrific."

I've never had any reason to change any of those opinions.

I should record here the involvement of Marvin Miller, who is one of my favorite people. He didn't show up at the Commissioner's office by accident. I wanted him there, and the Commissioner knew he was coming. Indeed, Miller and he had discussed the meeting at the Curt Flood trial, which was then in process. Miller suggested lunch. The Commissioner didn't want to be seen in public with us. I think he was right to want a secret meeting. I also think his best friends are probably his worst enemies.

Before the hearing, Miller had received some flack—not only from the baseball establishment, but also from players. One player representative, good old Moe Drabowsky of Kansas City, called to say the team had passed a resolution against the book. (I can't imagine why he was so upset about *Ball Four* unless it was the fact that we misspelled his name in it.) "What do you want me to do about it?" Miller asked. Moe said he didn't know. Which to Miller was exactly the point. He expresses it this way: "First of all, Dick Moss and I went to the hearing because every player is entitled to due process. If there is any possibility of a charge against him on the particular situation of writing a book, it seems to me that you've got one redress. You can recognize that he's entered a new arena, that he's written a book, and is now subject to all kinds of criticism. If you don't like his book, don't like his style, you can say so. That's fair game. But to say that there is just cause for disciplinary action within the Players Association for having written it, well, that gets into a whole new area and must be challenged. I heard threats that someone was going to punch him in the nose. He'll have to defend himself against that. But one thing I never heard is someone say the book is a pack of lies. That's an interesting omission."

Bless you, Marvin Miller.

4.

SANCTITY OF THE CLUBHOUSE

There were two arguments against the writing and publication of *Ball Four* that seemed particularly cogent. At least two that got to me most. The first, although sometimes stated in somewhat different ways, always came down to "violating the sanctity of the clubhouse." Sanctity of the clubhouse. Has a ring to it. Sounds like it's right up there with the sanctity of the confessional, or the sanctity of the lawyer-client, physician-patient relationship. I suppose baseball players and sports writers, a great many of them anyway, actually believe there is such a thing. Somebody, though, was showing a bit of tongue in-cheek posting one of those loose-letter cafeteria menu signs in the Cincinnati Reds' clubhouse about the time of the playoffs. The sign read:

> What you see here
> What you hear here

Let it stay here
When you leave here

This is a routine sign and you see the same
sort of sentiment hung in a lot of clubhouses.
Only this one was signed. The bottom line said:
Jim Bouton.

Fair enough. The question, intentional or not,
that this sign somewhat ruefully posed is whether there really is a sanctity of the clubhouse.
After all, what's a clubhouse? It's a place for
men to change their pants. In this place baseball
strategy (which may be as mythical as sanctity)
is sometimes discussed. In this place a manager
may give a pep talk to his players, or perhaps
berate one for poor performance. (If he does,
though, he will lose points, for berating is supposed to be done in the "privacy of the manager's office." This is almost as sanctified as the
clubhouse.)

So what I want to know is what's so damn
important or secret about what goes on in a clubhouse? The only reason to keep any of it secret
is, of course, that most of it is silly. Nothing happens in clubhouse meetings. Nothing happens in
clubhouses. I suppose if I really wanted to vi-
olate the "sanctity of the clubhouse" I could have
quoted all the bastards who use the word "nig-
ger" on supposedly happily integrated teams. I
could have recorded the stupid anti-Semitic

remark. I could have shown, in much more detail, the mindlessness of it all.

A clubhouse is not a CIA office. If what happens in a clubhouse gets out, nobody will be shot, no wars will be caused, no one will die, no one will even get sick, except maybe from laughing. When it is revealed that Gary Bell says he's going to pitch every opposition batter by "smoking him inside," and that he is taken seriously, no one is hurt. Why should that remain secret? That's *education*.

One of my nose-to-nose confrontations with Dick Young, leading exponent of clubhouse sanctity, journalistic division, went like this:

ME: Who did I hurt? I mean, who the hell did I hurt?

YOUNG: Well, you hurt a whole lot of ballplayers.

ME: How the hell did I hurt them?

YOUNG: Now they have to go to their wives and say, yes, it's true that airline stewardesses stay in the same hotels and some of the guys fool around with them. And they have to convince their wives that *they* don't. Maybe you have to convince your wife about something that never happened in the first place.

ME: All I know is that if I caused any man to have serious problems with his wife, he couldn't have had a very good relationship with her in the first place. I mean, could the book cause you any trouble with *your* wife?

YOUNG: Yeah, I'd have some troubles.

ME: Well for crying out loud. What kind of relationship do you have with your wife?

YOUNG: A jealous one.

In the immortal words of Phil Rizzuto, holy cow. Is *that* what caused all the flack?

What I find hard to believe is that in this era of sexual freedom and enlightenment, a woman can send her husband on the road and worry about what he's doing there. You either trust your husband or you don't. You either stay married or you get a divorce. But you can't live on the razor's edge. You can't let what somebody says in a book seriously affect your life. If you have any kind of head, you've probably imagined much worse than anything that was said or even hinted at in *Ball Four*. I know there are naïve baseball wives. Yet I can't help thinking that if they're so naïve as to be affected by the foolishness I recorded in *Ball Four,* they probably couldn't read in the first place.

It's interesting, by the way, that the reaction of baseball wives expressed to me, directly or indirectly, was always positive. It's true a wife isn't likely to walk up to me and punch me in the nose. So I don't figure to get many negative reactions. But I got a lot of nice comments from wives, and many players, even some of those who told me they hated the book, abashedly admitted their wives loved it, spent half the night reading it and giggled all the way through it.

Theory: Women like sexy men. A lot of wives enjoyed the idea of their husbands being so sexy they crawled around on rooftops hoping to get a glimpse of a naked lady.

And something else: I haven't heard of a single divorce caused by *Ball Four*. Despite what Dick Young thinks, I don't believe I ever will. Even now that it is out in paperback.

Now I think I should take this opportunity to complete the recording of the long discussion I had with Young. All of it may not be directly pertinent, but I think the world should know.

ME: You know who's listening to you? The hard-hat types, that's who, the dum-dums, the kind of people who write obscene letters and don't have the guts to sign their names. Those are the people who agree with you and send me your columns with obscenities scrawled across them.

On the other hand, I'm getting a lot of really good letters, letters from businessmen who have secretaries, letters from people who care, neat, thoughtful letters, and all of them are signed. Those are the kind of people who are on my side.

YOUNG: Are you trying to generalize about hard-hats? What's the matter with hard-hats? I happen to know some very nice hard-hats.

I told him I was sure he did. And then my

mind made one of its tricky leaps to a line Young had in a column about the hippie-types who picketed Kuhn's office when I was called in. Young had himself calling up the receptionist and asking if the protesters were boys. And the lady, he wrote, answered: "I think so."

ME: What were you trying to show there?

YOUNG: I was just trying to show the type of person who thinks you're a hero.

ME: So you're generalizing about kids with long hair. And I can't generalize about hard-hats. Obviously what you think is fair for you, you don't think is fair for me.

We chewed that around for a while and then I attacked from another direction.

ME: A lot of people who read books for a living are going to read this book, and what are you going to be saying if those reviews are good? If they think I've used poor taste or poor judgment or cheated anybody or hurt anybody, they're going to be pointing that out. But they won't. (I knew that because Shecter had promised.) I haven't hurt anybody. I just said a bunch of things you wish *you* had said. And you don't like me doing that.

Besides, you used to write nice things about me. You even said once you admired me. How come you changed?

YOUNG: I changed because you're a different person now than you were when you were a winner. You're a loser now and you're down and out and you've become bitter.

ME: Bitter? For crissakes, any writer who's known me through the years always remarks how I've managed to stay the same, win or lose. Anyway, I don't consider myself a loser.

YOUNG: Well, you're not exactly sure of your position, are you?

ME: Maybe not, but I'm a major league ballplayer. How many major league ballplayers are there in the whole country, six hundred? I'm probably higher up in my profession than you are in yours. Are you one of the top six hundred writers in the country?

I'm not particularly proud of that one. I get that way in the heat of battle. Dick Young is a major league writer. I wouldn't let that stop me from arguing with him, though. Like at one point, as I jabbed my incisive questions at him, he said, "What's this, an inquisition?" I had him there too.

ME: Crissakes, Dick, for a guy who's been asking tough questions for thirty years, you're getting kind of uppity when someone starts questioning Dick Young.

He calmed down. And later on he went so far as to admit: "I'm not saying it won't be an interesting book. The only thing I say is that you've violated the moral code. What does your wife think when she reads that stuff?

ME: My wife and I have a healthy relationship. That stuff doesn't mess her up at all.

And you know something? I don't think Young was so concerned about the sanctity of the clubhouse, or about messing up ballplayers with their wives because of stewardesses. I think what he really was concerned about was his certain knowledge that if a best-selling book about baseball was going to be written, he should have written it. That, and his jealous wife.

The second argument that touched off the most reaction in me was somewhat more philosophical, and more difficult to handle. Eventually almost all the rock throwers got around to it. The argument is this: When a reporter or writer goes into a clubhouse, talks to a player, a manager, he has a notebook in his hand. Everybody knows what he's doing there. If there's something someone doesn't want in print, he doesn't have to say anything. But nobody knew I was writing a book. Writing, so far as baseball people were concerned, was not my business. Therefore they felt it was perfectly all right to behave naturally around me. Then I turned out to be a secret enemy in camp.

I have to admit that this argument messed up my mind for a while. No one likes to feel like a sneaky little rat, which is, no matter how it's phrased, the thrust of this proposition. On reflection, however, there are two things I can say —not so much in defense as in explanation. First, most everybody on the team *knew* I was writing a book. I was forever taking notes. At first I kidded about writing my "memoirs—some day." Later on, after I told a couple of roommates, after I left a pen on the back of the mound one inning, it was, by and large, understood that I was doing a book about *now*. In fact, guys would come up to me and say, "Here's a good story for your book." Or somebody would say, "Put that in your book, Bouton."

So I wasn't that much of a spy after all.

Secondly, there is this. Does a man have the right to write everything that's in his own head? These things happened to me, or to other people when I was around. They became part of whatever there is inside my head. Do I not own what's there just because I'm not a professional writer? If I do not, then no politician can write an autobiography, no actor can recount his adventures behind the scenes, no doctor can write about what it takes to make a surgeon. I suppose Thomas Wolfe shouldn't have written *Look Homeward, Angel* because he hadn't told anyone in his hometown he was doing it. When Joe McGinniss was writing *The Selling of the President* everybody knew he was this young, innocent-looking writer. They also were somehow certain he was *for* Richard Nixon. Did McGinniss betray the sanctity of the political clubhouse? Not a bit.

I really think that what blew so many minds

was that I wrote a book about sports that was funny, irreverent, even grammatical; me, the jock with the blond hair and blue eyes. Couldn't have written it for fun and games. Must be something deeper. That's it—the greedy bastard wrote it for money.

Baseball people come up with things like that because they're laying their own values on me. They ask themselves, "Why would *I* do a thing like that?" And the answer comes back: money. Whenever anybody comes to a ballplayer with a proposition or a project, the first thing the player wants to know is how much money is going to be in it for him. Yet the guy who wrote *Ball Four* for money, the guy with the deep, greedy eyes, is the same one who argued in the clubhouse that anyone who wanted to should be able to speak at a dinner for $25 when everybody else was insisting that $150 should be the minimum. If I was as greedy as the rest of them I'd have been insisting on $150 too. And I'd have gotten it a lot quicker than most of the others.

One of the things *Ball Four* was called a lot was "kiss and tell." I insisted it wasn't. I said I drew a line, that anything I thought would cause a divorce I left out. Actually, I was kidding about that. I honestly felt there was nothing to the sex in *Ball Four* that should or would disturb a healthy marriage, or even a marriage with a little sinus condition. What I think happened is that once rumors about *Ball Four* got around, rumors that it was going to tell all about everything about everybody, six hundred guys went home and confessed. Now *that* can disturb a marriage.

Actually I think I may have helped some marriages. Several Baseball Annies told me I had ruined it for them. The players' wives were making all the trips. Indeed, shortly after publication, Ralph Houk discovered that practically every Yankee wife had made the trip to Washington. He blamed *Ball Four*.

Finally, about the personal (translate: sexual) side of sanctity of the clubhouse. A lot of guys brag around clubhouses about their recent conquests, often in great detail. Despite ugly rumors to the contrary (no doubt started by people who didn't read the book), I never quoted them. I did use some sex stories, and I did use a lot of names. But you could look it up—I clearly didn't use names in the sex stories, at least not in the incriminating ones. The fact that a bunch of guys talk about sex in the clubhouse and kid about beaver shooting (which is merely girl watching on a more scientific level) is hardly startling news. Yet if there are interesting or amusing things said, it hurts no one to reveal them.

I used a story in *Ball Four* about Fred Talbot being served with fake paternity-suit papers as a practical joke. The fact that this disturbed him was taken by some to mean that he must have put himself into compromising positions. Even Talbot felt that way.

"How the hell am I going to keep my wife from reading that goddam book?" Talbot said to my friend, Mike Marshall.

"He's got it in there that you're innocent," Marshall said.

"Yeah," Talbot said, "but you're guilty when you just get into one of those things. I'll never be able to explain to my wife it was a joke."

To which another one of my friends, Steve Hovley, said, "The book will probably cause a lot of players to have heart-to-heart talks with their wives. It'll be a good thing."

Me, I think that Talbot's wife should understand that, at least on the basis of what was printed in *Ball Four*, her husband is as pure, maybe purer, than new-fallen Tibetan snow. The story about Talbot was not told as a sexy one. It was merely an example of the rough, practical-joke humor one encounters in the clubhouse. And I don't care what anybody says. It *was* funny.

So is this story about Dick Radatz. You may think it's merely kinky, yet it reflects accurately on several aspects of clubhouse life—the kind of things baseball players are liable to get innocently involved in, the kind of things we might be willing to do, and the kind of things we laugh at. I tell you, this is a clubhouse thigh slapper.

Radatz is the guy who had a quick, sensational career with the Red Sox as a relief pitcher. The way he tells it, he got talked into going up to this fellow's apartment. And then the guy explained what he wanted. "He broke out a couple of crates of oranges," Radatz said, "took off his clothes, stood up against the wall and told me to throw the oranges at his ass. Christ, he'd give me a hundred bucks every time I went up there. Just to throw oranges at his ass. Sometimes the oranges weren't too ripe and they'd really open up some welts on him. Those were my peak years, too, when I could really bring it. He loved it."

Now about Tony Kubek. If I had told this story in *Ball Four* it would have been called some kind of dirty betrayal. The only reason I didn't, was I forgot. Since the book came out, though, I've talked to Tony about it and asked him how he'd feel if I ran it in this book. He said fine, I think. When Kubek played in the Evangeline League his roommate was named Dominick Maisano. Kubek was from Wausau, Wisconsin, and Maisano was from Brooklyn, which means that Maisano, although he couldn't have been more than twenty-one, was at least fifteen years older than Kubek. At any rate, one of the local sports was to hang around outside the hotel and say dirty things to a couple of homosexuals who used to cruise the neighborhood. Not for Tony, of course. He was always up in his room, drinking a milkshake, reading *Field and Stream.*

So one day Maisano talked one of the homosexuals into going up to the room to visit Kubek. He gave him the key and said, "Look, there's this big, tall, good-looking guy in the room and you can go up there and do your thing with him. The problem is that he's a little shy—young and nervous, you know? But he's willing, so don't be put off. He just has to be talked into it. Don't take no for an answer. Keep persuading him and he'll come around."

The homosexual goes upstairs, unlocks the door and walks in on Tony. In about ten minutes, I'm told, Tony was quivering in a corner of the room, holding the guy off with a chair, like he was a lion. And the guy didn't give up until Maisano came upstairs and called him off.

Finally, there's the kind of sex story people *think* I included in *Ball Four* and really didn't.

This one is about a famous young pitcher at an afternoon gang bang. He was, shall we say, in the middle of his turn, when one of the older pitchers tapped him on the back and said, "Don't come, kid, you're pitching tonight." The kid swears he didn't. And I swear never to tell his name. After this appears, however, there are certain guys on a certain ball club who are going to go around telling this kid's name. A pox on them.

5

TELLING IT LIKE IT ISN'T

When Larry Dierker, pitcher, Houston Astros, very good, was doing his two-week reserve stint at an army camp in Virginia, he got a call from a guy who worked for a local newspaper. The guy said he understood that all the Astro wives were upset about *Ball Four*. "What does your wife think about it and what is your feeling about it?" No comment, Larry Dierker said. "I won't talk about the book."

The nicest thing would have been if Dierker had said his wife loved it, he loved it and get lost. Actually he was ambivalent about the book. He felt I had every right to say whatever I wished. At the same time he would not have said that kind of thing himself. So he wasn't going to praise the book. Nor was he going to rip it.

What's bad about all this is that the newspaper guy was looking for a rip. Look, I understand how newspapers work and a lot of my friends are newspapermen. I don't agree with Spiro Agnew that the only news is good news. Yet a lot of bad things happen when a reporter sets out with a story already written inside his head. He is in fact acting as a roadblock between the public and the truth. There's something vaguely sad and at the same time hackle-raising about Marty Martinez, the Astro utility man, coming over to me and saying, "I always said something nice when they asked me about the book, but they never put what I said in the newspapers."

I can get pretty paranoid about baseball. I don't believe, however, there was a newspaper conspiracy against *Ball Four*. A lot of sports writers didn't like it, of course, and this was their obvious right. Yet there were things in newspapers that were, well, bad.

Take this one. The dean of American sports journalism is Red Smith. That is, he's counted as the dean, although a lot of attitudes have changed about sports in recent years and Red Smith hasn't changed very much. (Once in a while, though, he can still surprise you.) At any rate, Red Smith wrote he didn't like *Ball Four*. He wrote it was a bad book.

> The complaint here is that it is sometimes dull, sometimes annoying, and frequently in bad taste. This probably isn't the fault of Bouton alone. Chances are his editor is also to blame.

That's what he wrote. But what he said to a

man who is his friend is that he *never read the book*. He was angry, he said, at the editor because of an article written by him in *Esquire* critical of Vince Lombardi. Red Smith counted Vince Lombardi as a good friend. Therefore, *Ball Four* couldn't have been a good book. Got it?

Then we have the sports writer who wrote about *Ball Four* according to the way he thought the wind was blowing. A lot of guys around the country write *all* their sports that way. It's a form of public pandering, as insulting as it is dishonest.

An example of this genre was available in the Denver *Post* from a man named Jim Graham. On May 20, just about the time the first *Look* excerpt appeared, Graham wrote that "baseball à la Bouton really is a funny game." And he quoted a lot of the funny passages. He was plainly delighted by the whole thing.

By June 3, after *Ball Four* had become what everybody likes to call "controversial," there was a change in Graham's attitude. On that date he wrote:

> What makes a guy like Bouton pop off that way in print?
> Could be a deep-seated kiss-and-tell complex, I suppose, or maybe it's just the lure of the almighty buck.

Certainly the old clubhouse rule, "What you say here, and what you see here, let it stay here," has gone by the boards.

They've hardly played the last inning before some flake is out with a book with one of those inside stories, giving his teammates the rip.

The real foolishness here is that if everybody was telling what went on in baseball, there would have been no sensation around *Ball Four.* What we'd been getting in sports writing, with certain exceptions, was nice, plain gruel. There was a marvelous line on this subject in a *New York Times* column by Bob Lipsyte involving Red Holzman, the coach of the New York Knickerbockers. Holzman had just had a book ghosted for him about his championship season. "Excuse me," he was quoted as saying. "I got to go check my proofs to make sure I didn't say anything about anybody."

Now we have Carl Yastrzemski's comment on how a sports book should be written (as opposed to the way I had written mine). "I went down to Miami with a bunch of questions Al Hirschberg had given me and I answered them into a tape recorder. It took me just three days."

Now you know about sports books, at least sports books like Carl Yastrzemski's.

The reason that kind of baseball book is so

easy to find is simply this: Baseball players think, "The game's been nice to me. I'm fine. I'm happy. Don't rock the boat. You take care of me, I'll take care of you. Who cares if anyone knows what the game is really like? Let's keep our mouths shut so we can all make a good buck."

Jack Mann had an interesting talk with Darold Knowles of the Senators in his Washington *Daily News* column on just this point.

"Look," Knowles said, "he [Bouton] says Yastrzemski 'has a bit of dog in him.' Everybody knows that, but you don't say it."

Why don't you, if it's true? "Because of the fans," Knowles said. "We're in the baseball business. We have to keep up the image of the game."

The game, it follows logically, has a phony image. "Hell, yes, it does," Knowles said. "Do you know a business that doesn't?"

It was disappointing, too, to discover that sports reporters and columnists could be so blinded by rage about *Ball Four* that they were prevented from exerting even a minimum of journalistic energy before leaping into print with denunciation. I think, for example, of Joe Falls of the Detroit *Free Press*. Joe thought the book was, in his word, horseshit. That's okay. But one of the big reasons he thought it was horseshit was the story I had told about Gary Bell's wife calling him at four in the morning only to be told by his roommate that he was out playing golf.

Falls deduced from this that I had probably caused serious problems between Bell and his wife. What he apparently refused to read in *Ball Four*, although it was right there, was that *Nan Bell told the story in the first place.* She told it to a group of players and their wives over dinner. She told it because it was funny. And her bottom line about Gary being on the golf course in the middle of the night was, "Well, maybe he was." That was in *Ball Four* too. And I wonder why Falls insisted upon misreading it.

Apparently Falls wasn't the only one. I gave a little talk to some kids at the Bogota (N.J.) high school, and during the question period one of them asked: "You said in your book that when Gary Bell's wife called, he was in bed with some girl. Now don't you think you went too far in revealing something like that?" The kid got a two-minute lecture on how to read instead of letting a dirty mind run away. He deserved it.

And here's how the trouble I really didn't have with Tommy Davis developed. Davis has a put-on sense of humor. It's a humor of exaggerated ill-feeling and a fairly popular form around baseball. Like I'd walk by him and he'd say, "Get away from me, don't touch me. You're trouble." Or he'd say: "My wife called me from L.A. today. She wants to know what stewardesses I'm going out with and who I'm kissing on the bus. What's she going to say when she reads the book?" And one time we were kidding around and he got me into a happy, giggling headlock and said, "You son of a bitch, if you said anything about me in that book I'm going to knock your block off." Anyone who hangs around clubhouses (and a lot of people who don't) would understand that this was roughhouse kidding. But there was a reporter in the room who couldn't—or wouldn't—understand. The result was that Davis' kidding line turned up on the wire services, meaning all over the country, as a serious one.

Now Joe Durso of *The New York Times*. Actually this is somewhat less about Durso than it is about Elston Howard. The thing is that Elston Howard took it personally. I'm not altogether sure why, except there was a certain irrationality about his reaction, and irrationality is often the product of fear. "Ellie's kind of worried about the book," one of my spies on the Yankees told me. "He's starting to get things set up in advance—that you're not telling the truth. I guess he doesn't want anybody to believe what you say about him."

It must have taken Howard some time to get to this point, for the first time I saw him, when Houston was playing an exhibition game with the Yankees in the Astrodome, he was smiling broadly. "Hey Bouton, I hear you wrote a book," he said. "That's going to be *something*. And you did it with Shecter too. Boy, I got to read that thing."

Even before he read it, though, he was trying to rewrite it. A lot of the players on the Yankees were, I was told, nervous. "They're all trying to think if they ever did something mean to you," Curt Blefary told me. But Howard was in there pushing reconstructed anecdotes. One day he told about how I had attacked Frank Crosetti, the coach; how I had reached into his locker, pulled him out by his uniform and started punching him. It was Fritz Peterson who interrupted. "No, no, Ellie. You got it all wrong. Bouton didn't do anything but yell. Then Cro jumped up and started beating on him. All Bouton did was cover up and laugh."

Nice to know there are still friendly truthtellers around.

I don't blame Elston Howard for not liking *Ball Four*. I was tough on him, although not as tough, I suspect, as he thought I was going to be. In any case, he let loose a series of tirades against me in the Yankee dugout. Each time, though, he carefully went around to the newspapermen present and asked them not to put any of it in the paper. Well, one day Joe Durso went home early.

The result was a column that managed to illuminate some of the secret corners of Elston

Howard's mind (and possibly Joe Durso's too). I'll not attempt to refute most of the material in it because what Ellie said had a lot of built-in self-destruct. I will, though, point out one amusing section. It had to do with something that happened in 1963, the year I won twenty-one games. The quote from Howard via the Durso column:

"Once we were fighting for the pennant late in September and he had 19 victories, but this day he was being rocked good. So Ralph Houk took him out, and later Jim said, 'I guess he didn't want me to win 20.' Do you think Houk cared how many games he won as long as he won the pennant?"

Now I do not insist that every newspaperman check every statement made to him. There's very little time for that sort of thing in the newspaper business. Yet I can't help believing that if Durso had taken the trouble to check the box score and story of this particular game (it wouldn't have been difficult; I only won twenty once), severe doubt might have been cast on everything else Howard said. Perhaps then he would have hesitated to run the column. Perhaps that's why he didn't want to check. If he had, this is what he would have discovered.

I *was* going after my twentieth. In fact, though, it was *early* in September (the ninth).

I had plenty of time to get it. And it was *some* pennant race. We had a thirteen-and-a-half-game lead on that day and when I did win my twentieth, on my *next* start (September 13) we clinched the pennant. It was one of the earliest clinchings in history.

Before the game in question I had been down with a virus and consequently was feeling terrible. But I was winning. The score was 6–0. I must really have been getting rocked.

In the seventh inning (the game was played in Kansas City) I gave up two hits. Houk came out and told me there was no use struggling; I was sick, the game was wrapped up, and we had some fine relief pitchers ready to finish it for me. I couldn't have agreed more and told Houk so. In came Steve Hamilton.

With me in the clubhouse, incredulity growing like a snowball rolling down a mountain, my friend Hamilton slowly and with great effort permitted the A's to tie the score. It didn't take much. Say three walks and a home run. I've done it myself—many times. In the eighth, Hal Reniff gave up the winner. We lost it, 7–6.

If anybody asked, what the hell could I say? Obviously that somebody didn't want me to win twenty. Maybe somebody up there. It's my kind of line. Howard should have understood that. And even if he didn't, Durso should. I can only believe he didn't want to.

Just in case anybody gets the mistaken notion that I want to deprive the press of any of its rights, I should tell about Houston's great bus put-off. It got a lot of space in the papers and at one point the knock was put on one J. Bouton for attacking his newspaperman friends. It's a funny story and it goes back a lot longer than a lot of people know.

It all started with an anonymous player's wife who called the Houston Astros and asked them what they could do about getting her husband home at a decent hour after home games. In order not to reveal who the player was, we'll call him Jimmy Wynn. The problem was that this call got into the newspapers. It caused a lot of comment, especially by the wives. As a result, the players got angry. Who could they get angry at? Jimmy Wynn? His wife? Their own wives? Nope. They got angry at the newspapermen.

That wasn't all of it. The worst part was we were also losing games. Not simply. We were getting our asses beaten. There was a lot of tension, compounded somewhat by the newspaper response to *Ball Four*. It hung over the club like smog over Los Angeles.

So we had a meeting and Denny Lemaster said, "All right, how many guys want to keep the sports writers off the bus?" A bunch of guys raised their hands. So Lemaster says, "All right, that's it; they're off the bus." It was like voting for player representative. All right, who wants to be player rep? You? Okay, you're it. That was the meeting.

Now Denny goes to the reporters and says it was a unanimous vote. This put me in a very interesting position. Every wise-ass in the country said I voted to keep the writers off the bus because I wanted to keep the good quotes for myself. (Not a bad idea. I wish I had thought of it.) When questioned about it, I said, "Of course, the writers have to be kept off the bus. They've got no business sneaking around, listening to what guys say and writing it down."

When the news of the bus ban got into the newspapers and on the wires, we got an angry telegram from Dick Young—a two-page job. He wrote it on behalf of the Baseball Writers Association and he said precisely what he should have said—since when do writers on a bus cause the team to lose? A perfect question.

Pretty soon we were being called, accurately, crybabies. So I suggested that we issue the following statement:

As a result of our winning performance tonight it has been decided unanimously to continue the ban of writers from the bus on a game to game basis.

That was if we won. If we lost, I thought we should issue this:

Tonight's loss proves that the writers have not been the cause of our earlier losses. So starting tomorrow, we're going to allow the writers on our bus. However, we are going to bar our infielders in order to find out if they're the cause.

I further suggested that after subsequent losses we bar outfielders, pitchers, catchers, coaches, manager—until we found the right combination. For some reason, Lemaster didn't think this was a good idea.

We all were made to look very foolish in the papers around the country. Our pride wounded, we had another meeting and the writers were allowed back on the bus. It worked, because we didn't lose any more than we had before the big ban. On the other hand, we didn't win any more either.

It wasn't just the press that got on me. A whole bunch of baseball guys knocked me to reporters. The San Diego team burned my book on the clubhouse floor in Los Angeles just before the Houston club got there, leaving the ashes and a recognizable binder.

Bob Gibson of the St. Louis Cardinals said I was stabbing people in the back.

Lee Maye of the Washington Senators said I had a good chance to get my head busted.

George Brunet of who knows where said, "Suppose he causes a divorce with that damn book."

Jim Bunning of the Philadelphia Phillies said, "The thing that's wrong with the book is the thing that's wrong with the country."

Hank Soar, the umpire, said, "If we all wrote about what we know about other people there'd be no baseball."

Jim Turner, the Yankee pitching coach, said, "That book would go over great in Russia."

Yogi Berra said "professional people" wouldn't like the book. (Oh yes he did.)

Joe Cronin, president of the American League, said, "It's the most derogatory thing and the worst thing for baseball I've ever seen. He's got ballplayers sleeping with each other's wives. He's got them being Peeping Toms. He's even got them kissing each other. I've never read anything so bad in my whole life."

And Tug McGraw of the Mets said, "I think *Ball Four* is great reading. But suppose he was your roommate."

Mack Jones of the Montreal Expos peered over the dugout and said, "Which one is Bouton? I never met him."

A bystander, jokingly: "You will, in his book."

Jones, furiously: "If my name is anywhere in that book, he's going to get a punch in the mouth from me, I mean it."

Three things. One: Mack Jones wasn't in *Ball Four*. Two: Who the hell ever heard of Mack Jones? Three: He's in this one, and my mouth, I suppose, is available.

A letter. This one scrawled across a newspaper picture of me coming out of the Commissioner's office.

> You've got a lot of guts talking about the Yankees. If you weren't on the Yankees you'd have been horseshit like you are now. You'd make a maggot throw up.

It was signed "ex." I wasn't sure whether this was illiterate for X or actually meant "ex" of the Yankees. In any case, I have an idea who sent it. It was either Fred Talbot who was mentioned forty-eight times in *Ball Four*, or Bob Meyer, who wasn't mentioned at all. My reasoning is this. Both were in the Yankee chain. The letter was sent on stationery from a hotel in Des Moines and (1) they're both cheap, (2) they both spent a lot of time in Des Moines. One doubt, though. Neither was famous for his imagery. And the one about the maggot isn't bad.

There were a lot of people who seemed to have a dual attitude toward *Ball Four*. David Eisenhower had one kind. President Nixon's son-in-law commented on the book early on, presumably after reading only the magazine excerpts, which were deliberately tough. "He's a sensitive observer," David Eisenhower said. Then, after the book had been published, he said, "Bouton has a certain flair and charm that makes the book readable, but he doesn't have the writing talent to maintain interest. In fact, after about 250 pages I just had to give it up. [Nixon doesn't get his call until page 321.] Yes, the book will sell, but I don't understand what Bouton thinks he's accomplishing. Is this the way to add color to the game? I don't think so. I don't see the book as being good for baseball, so I don't see the purpose. Besides, locker rooms just aren't like that."

There was also Bob Gibson's kind. Gibson seemed to be tremendously offended by the book. I can't understand why. Perhaps it was because he hadn't read it. ("It's a horseshit book," said Billy Martin. "I didn't read it, but I know it's horseshit. My wife read it. She thought it was great.") What I resented most about Gibson was his saying that I stabbed people in the back. I half hoped that when I ran into him we'd have a discussion about it—calm, reasoned and shouting.

The first time I encountered Gibson he was in the outfield of the St. Louis ball park and I was running some laps.

"Hi Bob," I said.

"Hi Jim," he said.

Well, maybe he had me confused with some other Jim. So I went by him again, slower.

"Hi Bob," I said.

"Hi Jim," he said.

I couldn't believe it. I decided to try one more time.

"Hi Bob, how's your wife's book going?"

"Too early to tell."

Talk about confrontations.

Another typical encounter was with Joe Garagiola. I have to give Joe credit. He was on *Ball Four*, both on the Today show and his Monitor radio show, right from the beginning. He read the book in proof and he asked a lot of good questions. But at the same time he was telling me how much he admired my guts for writing the book, he was taking every opportunity to call me fink for doing so. Joe Garagiola didn't get to be a star in broadcasting by planting himself firmly on only one side of a question.

Let me start this off by telling you a little about Joe Pepitone. During the All-Star break we both took a late plane out of Houston for New York. I was going there to do some TV appearances for the book and my tab was being picked up. Joe was going there, I'm not sure what for; possibly to straighten out some of his marital difficulties, possibly to raise some money for his failing business. Anyway, there were about six people on the plane, five of them back in coach and one of them, Joe Pepitone, in first class. "What the hell are you doing flying second class?" Joe Pepitone says to me. There I am with three seats to myself, all the room in the world. So I say, "What the hell are *you* doing in first class?"

And Joe Pepitone says, with a giggle, "I *always* travel first class."

I guess he does, sort of. Mostly he travels in a world that's about fifteen degrees off the world the rest of us travel. He is desperately eager to be liked, for one thing, so he has a tendency to probe until he finds out what you want him to say, and then he says it.

I like Joe Pepitone. I played on the Yankees with him and minor league ball with him and enjoyed all of it, especially the time he stole an elevator in San Antonio. The hotel manager thought I was the one who did it, but I like Joe Pepitone anyway.

The fact is that Pepitone was often fun to be around. I remember the time we were coming off a two-week road trip and just before the plane landed a teammate said to him, "Jesus, Joe, you got lipstick all over your collar."

Pepitone looked down, nodded wisely, took off his sport jacket, took off his shirt, crumbled it into a ball and threw it away. Then he put his jacket on over his T-shirt.

At the airport the lady asked Pepitone how come he wasn't wearing a shirt. Peppy snapped his fingers, looked rueful and said what the hell, two weeks on the road, thirteen shirts, bad planning.

I liked Pepitone even more than usual the day he came over to me in the clubhouse and said, "Hey, I hear the Yankees are upset about the book." He was touching his hair (or hairpiece, I guess) a lot, the way he does, and smiling the smile I'm sure he thinks looks evil, but is more boyish than anything else. "Well, listen, the hell with those guys—Mantle, Ford, Houk, all of them. They're all two-faced. None of them even called to say good-by when I was traded. I thought those guys were my friends. Bull. They just like you when you're going good. When you're not going good they don't want to have anything to do with you. You know who called me to tell me I was traded? Not Mike Burke, not Houk—Howard Berk, that's who. [Howard Berk's title with the Yankees is Vice-President of Administration.] So okay. You did your thing, you told the truth. Stick by it."

Thanks Joe, that was sweet.

Except that as soon as people went to work on him he changed his mind.

"Hey Joe, isn't it terrible about what Bouton said about Mantle?"

"Yeah, how about that son of a bitch? Where's he get the nerve to say that stuff about Mantle?"

That's the way the process works. I know, because Pepitone told me so. When Dick Young quoted him as saying I was "the horniest bleep" in baseball, I went right to him and asked what the hell. And Pepitone said, "Oh, I didn't say that. He misinterpreted. What I said was, you know, everyone screws around on the road and has a good time and Bouton likes to have a good time as much as anybody and how come he didn't write about himself? That's all I said. Dick just said it his own way."

A further ambivalence. When the book came out, Pepitone wanted to discuss the hilarious incident in it where he puts a piece of popcorn under his foreskin and goes to the Yankee doctor complaining of a new disease. "Listen, Jim," Pepitone said. "You think you could change that to *two* pieces of popcorn?"

Still, once in a while Pepitone could really lean on my irritation button. Once it had to do with Jimmy Wynn, who is the Mickey Mantle of the Houston club. (I guess he's sort of the Norman Mailer of baseball now that his wife has stabbed him.) Wynn got hit with a pitched ball. It just hit the peak of his batting helmet, but Jimmy, who is the kind of guy who can be out of action for a week with an upset stomach, gave it the full treatment. He went down in a heap like he had been hit by a boulder and then, when he discovered that the cap had dug into his eyelid and caused a slight cut, he went into another big act. They almost carried him from the field.

I was standing in the dugout at the time, and I said, "Boy, this guy is better than Joe Pepitone," knowing that Joe was standing right there. "He joins Joe Pepitone as a nominee for the Academy Award." Not brilliant, although obviously meant to be funny.

So now Wynn comes out of the ball game. It's not really the kind of injury that should knock him out of the game, but that's Wynn. When he gets to the dugout, Pepitone says, "Hey, Jimmy, come over here a minute. Bouton was on you. He said you were putting on an act."

"Now wait a minute," I said. "That was meant to be a joke, Joe, and you know it. I said it in front of you and said Jimmy was just like you. Don't try to get me in trouble."

Wynn, however, decided he wanted to take the whole thing seriously, maybe because he felt guilty about coming out of the game. And he really got on me. "Don't ever let me hear you say any fucking thing about me or I'll . . ." etc., etc. It was a real stupid, uptight scene. And it ended with Wynn saying, "You're the kind of guy who'd write this in a book."

Well, yes.

Still and all, in addition to liking Joe, I'm grateful to him. If it weren't for Joe Pepitone, my baseball career probably would have been shorter by many weeks. He kept taking the pressure off me. Every time I got into trouble, there was Peppy, in worse.

Example: The day I had that terrible game against the Mets and I thought the world was falling apart for me, Pepitone showed up at the park hung over out of his mind. That was sort of unusual, because Joe could hold his booze pretty good. This day, though, he was late getting to the ball park and he simply wasn't able to play. So he went to sleep on the rubbing table and after we got beat, and I thought Harry Walker would be getting on me between games, there was Pepitone to get on instead. Harry really screamed at him. Got all over his ass. Not only that, the players were all mad at him too. Nobody said a word to me, and I'd done a pretty good job of destroying that first game. The upshot was that Harry told Pepitone he'd play in the second game if he had to crawl out there. Joe had a great game, hit a home run, and got another hit. Which shows you something or other.

The next time Pepitone helped me out was during the All-Star break. Harry called a practice for the third day of the break (a not unprecedented, although last-minute move) and I went to him and said I couldn't make it. (I had a lot of TV stuff I was committed to do in New York those three days.)

"If you can't make it," Harry said, "we're going to have to suspend you."

"Gee whiz, Harry, that's a little severe, isn't it? Just for missing a workout? I mean, if I stayed out too late my wife wouldn't get a divorce, would she? She'd be angry, but she wouldn't get a divorce."

"Well, we can't be as flexible as a wife," Harry said. "We'll have to suspend you."

I wondered what he'd do if I missed a game, shoot me? But I just said, "Well, there's nothing I can do, Harry. I'm committed. I'm only in here telling you because I don't want you to be surprised when I don't show up."

I knew Pepitone was going to be in New York, too, and I asked him if he intended to return for the workout. "Nah," he said.

"Aren't you going to tell them?"

"Nah," Joe Pepitone said.

The result was that when I got back, I was fined a day's pay and $250. So was Pepitone, although his day's pay was a lot more than my day's pay. Besides that, Pepitone refused to pay or even show up to play anymore. So once again, the heat was off me. There must have been a half-dozen players who came up to me and said, "You know, we don't really mind you and your book and all that stuff. But Pepitone, that fucking Pepitone, he's too much."

This was the way Jim Owens, the pitching coach, put it: "I understand you had to go do that stuff in New York. But that Pepitone, he didn't even come tell us."

"You paying the fine?" I asked Pepitone in an idle moment.

"Nah," he said.

"How do you plan to get away with it?"

"My arm."

He'd been nicked by a pitched ball a few days before.

"Your arm?"

"Yeah, my arm still hurts, dig?"

In the end Pepitone was disbelieved, as he should have been. So he used that to demand to be traded. He said he couldn't play for a team that would accuse him of lying about an injury.

He was traded to Chicago and had a hell of a year there. I guess the Houston club didn't know how to treat Pepitone. They even tried to give him a roommate. Drove him right up the wall. When he was with the Yankees, Bruce Henry, the road secretary, would always be doing little things to make him feel like a big shot. Let's say Lee MacPhail, the general manager, was canceling out of a trip with the club at the last minute. Bruce would give Pepitone MacPhail's suite. "Joe, have a good time," he'd say. And Joe would live it up in the suite, and the next day he'd hit a home run and a couple of doubles.

Which is why when he jumped the Houston club I suggested that all the players chip in and buy an ad in the paper saying something like, "We all love you, Joe, and we need you. Please come back." What the hell, we had more chances to win with him than without him. Nobody would go for it. They thought it was a flaky idea. Maybe so. It might have worked, though.

I think the reason Pepitone did so well in Chicago was that some rich guy lent him a Rolls-

Royce for the season. Pepitone would pull up to the ball park, actually roll a red carpet out of the car, and walk into the place a foot off the ground. When he feels like a big man, Joe Pepitone's a big hitter. I think I'll miss him. Well, a little.

I should also say something here about my great roomie, Norm Miller. He was terrific all the way through. He read *Ball Four* in proof and said he thought it was great and funny and that he didn't think there was anything in there that should offend anybody at all. "When's the shit going to hit the fan?" he kept asking. "When we get to New York," I kept telling him. Sure enough, that's when it happened. The very first morning there was this pounding on the door. "Open up," this *voice* said. "This is Howaarddd Coselll. Open this door." We thought it might open by itself.

Miller opened the door and that famous nasal TV voice burst into the room complaining about baseball, the hotel, the world and winding up with, "Let's go, Bouton. We're on camera in ten minutes."

Miller just stood there with his jaw hanging open. And I loved his comment later. "Fuck him," Miller said. "If he was going to be like that I wouldn't even tell him who I was."

Anyway, Miller seemed to be having a ball. He went around with me to a lot of the TV stations, and later on, after he had heard me talking on the phone a lot, he would pick it up when it rang, say, "Yes, this is Jim Bouton," and answer the questions exactly as I would. He had it all down perfectly.

Then it happened. The date was June 5. The following day a reporter named Joe Heiling was going to have a story in the paper about how all the Astros felt about the book. I'd asked around a little bit about what some of the guys said to him and I was a little nervous. I didn't think things were going to come out very nicely. That night, needing reassurance, I asked Miller what he had told Heiling.

"I told him I admired your guts," Miller said. "You know, it takes a lot of courage for a guy to say the things you did and speak out like that. I said I got to hand it to you and you really deserve a lot of credit. I said I knew there were some things in there that are going to upset some people, but what the hell, you have a right to say it. It's a free world."

I was stunned. "Didn't you tell him you *loved* it? Didn't you tell him it was a riot? Didn't you tell him it was the greatest book you ever *read?*"

"Well, yeah. I told him it was funny. But you know, I was kind of afraid of what the front office might think. I mean, you know, I don't know how they're going to think about the book and I don't want to get on the wrong side of the front office."

In the immortal words of my favorite manager, Joe Schultz, aw shitfuck.

I tell the next series of anecdotes because they point up the single most hysterical reaction to *Ball Four*.

The first is about Doc Edwards, the Philadelphia catcher. He was one of the people who said he never read *Ball Four* because he knew he wouldn't like it. (Not that he was ever famous for reading books.) Anyway, one night in June in Philadelphia, Doc Edwards beat me a ball game. I came into it with the score 1–1 in the tenth. In the thirteenth he knocked in the winner by hitting a two-out knuckleball. Edwards said it was a pretty good knuckleball.

Naturally he was asked about *Ball Four*. "To me it's like breaking a marriage vow," Doc Edwards said. "Anything that happens in a clubhouse meeting, it stays there. Any incident that happens on the road, you keep it there. It's the way it's always been." (It's called, I think, the Major League Players Protective Association.)

Then he said: "They tell me he was pretty rough on Mickey Mantle and I don't think it was Bouton's place to do it. . . . The way I feel, Mantle put a lot of money in everybody's pockets—mine and Bouton's included. A lot more people around the American League came to see Mickey Mantle than came to see us."

It is interesting that despite all the noise made by baseball players about the book, there were no nose-to-nose confrontations. Elston Howard had at least three shots at me if he wanted them. Each time he sort of pretended neither he nor I was there. I gave Bob Gibson his chance and nothing happened. The only player who ever said anything harsh directly to me was Joe Torre of the Cardinals and he was in the stands and I was on the field at the time. The Cards were heading for the clubhouse from their bus when he spied me on the field. I didn't catch everything he said. It was something like this: "Hey, those were some nice things you said about Mantle. Watch out. I hear he's got a contract out on you."

Hah, I said. Hah, hah. To myself. Then I thought I'd better check things out with Joe Pepitone. "Listen, Joe. Can a guy go to the Mafia and buy a contract on you?"

Joe Pepitone was our local Mafia authority.

"Nah," he said. "There's only three reasons a Mafia guy will take you out. If you owe him money, and even then they don't like to kill you because dead men are lousy payers. So he'll probably just break your leg. If you're a Mafia guy yourself and you're trying to muscle in on his territory. He'll get you for that. The third way is if you're fooling around with his broad."

I decided I was safe. I don't fool around with broads. Anyway, Mafia broads.

Then there's this one. My brother told me that

one time, early on, one of the Cardinal announcers said, "And here comes Jim Bouton. He's the one who said those terrible things about Mickey Mantle. Isn't that something? Mantle's been in the game for fifteen years. He's had a lot of great seasons, and here's Jim Bouton, what's he ever done? Two good years and then nothing. Let's see how he does."

The guy must have been clairvoyant. The first thing I did was give up a double and the announcer said, "Well, look at that. Let's see him put *that* in his book."

And a letter on the bulletin board in the Astro clubhouse. It was hung up alongside a Dick Young column. It said:

> This item appeared in the New York *Daily News*. This reflects the view of most New Yorkers about Jim Bouton. We are sorry that Jim Bouton had the privilege of wearing the Yankee uniform and playing with THE GREAT MICKEY MANTLE. We can't help but think that if Jim Bouton spent less time keeping a diary and more time pitching, he might still be in a Yankee uniform. At the rate he is going, he might set a record for being on the roster of the most ball clubs.
>
> I guess you can classify him as an asset to your club, if not for his pitching ability then for the dissension he causes among your

ballplayers. Your team in a million years will never have a player as GREAT AS MICKEY.

The letter was signed, with some presumption, it seemed to me, "All New York Sports Fans." There was no other identification. The main question, though, was who put it up on the bulletin board. "Take that damn thing down," Jim Owens said when he saw it. Jimmy Ray said maybe Harry Walker put it up, but I didn't believe that. I never did find out who did it. I took it down, folded it, and put it in my pocket. Mike Marshall, who knows more than I do about a lot of things, said I shouldn't have. "It would have been cooler to just leave it up there," he said. Damn. I hate to lose my cool.

Now a dugout conversation:

PEPITONE: I never saw Mantle close a window on kids' hands.

BOUTON: I didn't say hands. I said he closed windows on kids. There's a difference.

PEPITONE: It's the way you said it.

BOUTON (*shrugging*): Argh.

GLADDING: Did you argue religion with Bobby Richardson?

BOUTON: We had a couple of minor discussions, very cordial. I used to argue religion a lot with Steve Hamilton.

PEPITONE: What about Ellie Howard? Everyone liked him.

BOUTON: He made it easy for people to like him. He never disagreed with anybody. He's the kind of guy who thought Bobby Richardson was a great person, and yet Bobby had his problems about black people.

PEPITONE: You mean he was prejudiced?

BOUTON: I didn't say that. But Bobby's church doesn't admit black people, and he believes blacks *want* to be separate. Steve Hamilton called it the only chink in his armor.

DON BRYANT: Would you let your daughter marry one?

BOUTON: She'll make her own choice.

GLADDING: Well, I guess I'm prejudiced then.

DILAURO (*to Pepitone, needling*): What about that column Joe Durso did with Ellie Howard. Was Howard right?

PEPITONE: Yeah, Howard was right.

DILAURO (*still needling*): Did Mantle *really* mess around?

BOUTON: Now wait a minute. I never said anyone messed around.

PEPITONE: You said they did and you didn't.

BOUTON: I used "we" all the way through. Can't you guys read?

GLADDING: Did Howard put mud on the ball for you?

BOUTON: Yeah, but it didn't help me. I wasn't

clever enough to make it work. I'd say, hey ump, I need a new ball. This one's all dirty.

JIMMY RAY (*among the audience*): Blood money.

GLADDING: How much are you going to make?

BOUTON: Probably a hundred thousand.

GLADDING: I thought you didn't do it for money.

BOUTON: I didn't know all this would happen. I expected to make $25,000 at the most.

PEPITONE: What difference does it make if Mantle doesn't sign the balls?

BOUTON: I think it says something about him.

PEPITONE: He makes too much money to sign balls.

BOUTON: That's all the more reason for him to sign them.

GLADDING: Yeah, but how come you didn't say something bad about yourself?

BOUTON: Listen, Fred. I said I used the word "we." And what about the time where I said it was three o'clock in the morning and I did a striptease and jumped into a swimming pool with a martini in each hand? What about that, Fred? What if I said that about you?

GLADDING: Well, it'd be a lie. I can't swim.

The thread here is obvious enough. It's Mickey Mantle. Nothing in *Ball Four* attracted as much noisy reaction as the few remarks I made about the man who has become a kind of American folk hero. What I said about Mantle was that I enjoyed his boyish charm, his country sense of humor, the warmth he exhibited to his teammates. I also said I didn't like it when I saw him brush aside young autograph-seekers and be nasty to newspapermen. And I suggested that he might have had an even more spectacular career had he slept more and loosened up with the boys at the bar less. You'd think I had desecrated the flag, knocked motherhood and attacked Spiro T. Agnew with an unabridged dictionary.

The regard in which Mantle is held by many in the country is as phenomenal as it is understandable. He is the perfect hero. Strong. Athletic. A man who overcame a disease which could still be fatal. Blond. Blue eyed. Perfect. At least he seems perfect and no one—or almost no one—wants to know any different. (I should point out that there have been other athletes as accomplished as Mantle, perhaps more so, who never attained his divinity. Of course, they were black.)

Time after time the Joe Garagiolas, the Frank Giffords, the Tony Kubeks would ask me why I wanted to destroy American heroes. Didn't the country *need* heroes?

My answer is that I didn't set out to destroy heroes. Anyway, it all depends on what your idea of a hero is. Why can't Mickey Mantle be a hero who has a bit too much to drink from time to time and cries into his glass that he will soon be dead, like his father and his uncle? Why do our heroes have to be so perfect and unflawed? In other parts of the world heroes can be drinkers or even wenchers and this only adds to their heroism.

That's one thing. The second is that I believe there are enough real heroes in America so that we don't have to kneel before fake ones. Athletic heroes are the least of America, not the most. Our kids would do a lot better to follow the career of Ralph Nader or Allard Lowenstein rather than Mickey Mantle or Roger Maris. (At last look Maris was selling beer, Mantle men's suits.)

There were some people, though, a surprisingly large number of them, who did not resent my remarks about Mantle. I don't know how many times people have come up to me right in the street and said I was exactly correct about Mantle. They all had the same story. Two, five, ten years ago, when they were little kids, they went up to Mantle when he was coming out of the Stadium and he rudely shoved them out of the way with, as they say, an oath. And then they went home and cried themselves to sleep.

Sample letter from a New York girl:

You know that I've been attending the Yankee games for quite a while, and I can honestly say that I too have witnessed Mantle, in particular, shatter the expectations of his young fans, so I was not particularly shocked by what you wrote, as the others seem to be.

In August I ran into Jeff Torborg, the Dodger catcher, and he said, "Liked what you've been saying about false heroes and about players not signing autographs. Some ballplayers really think they're God. I see Willie Davis walking through the people after games like he was some sort of king. I think it's important for everybody to sign for the fans. Especially the big stars."

We're not the only ones in baseball who think that. Recently, and after *Ball Four* came out, players were admonished by the Commissioner to sign autographs at all convenient times, even when in uniform, which was formerly against the rules.

As I've pointed out before, Mantle seldom showed the moody, dark side of his nature around the clubhouse. I mean not to his teammates. To them he was, largely, pleasant and amusing. Often he was up to his elbows in clubhouse games and practical jokes. Many times he went out of his way, as he did with me, to make rookies feel comfortable. Yet sometimes someone would bounce off him, hard, someone even like Joe Pepitone, a man who once said in the public prints that *I* didn't understand Mickey Mantle. This happened at the batting cage one of those times Mantle was injured and wanted to test his swing. Since he wasn't in the batting order he didn't have a turn, so he just walked up to the cage to hit. Ahead of Joe Pepitone. Except Pepitone said, "Fuck you, Mantle. After me."

Now that's the kind of thing you can say to a friend. And Pepitone always considered Mantle a friend. Mantle evidently wasn't feeling very friendly, though, for he stalked off to the clubhouse and didn't talk to Pepitone for a month. I mean not a word. There is nothing more silent than a Mickey Mantle silent treatment.

Then there was Jim Beauchamp. One day, not long after the book came out, he walked up to me and said, "Listen, I just want to tell you I'm not one of the guys who's mad at you for what you said about Mantle."

It turned out that when Beauchamp (pronounced Beechum) was just starting out in the St. Louis organization, he was at the St. Petersburg ball park that was shared by the Yankees and Cards. Mantle was behind the cage during batting practice and Beauchamp went up to him and said, "Hi Mickey, my name is Jim Beauchamp. I played football with your brothers. . . ." And Mantle got that flat, blank look in his eyes, turned on his heel and walked away.

Six months later, Beauchamp ran into Mantle again. He stuck out his hand, started his little speech and Mickey Mantle said, "Who gives a shit?"

"I actually said to myself," Beauchamp said, "that, well, Mickey must have had two bad days and I blundered into both. But it happened a *third* time. The same damn thing. And you know, I was a *ballplayer*, not just some fan, and he knew it."

I never expected anybody to complain to me that what I've said about Mickey Mantle isn't true. Not even Mantle would say that. I knew what people were *going* to say was, "Gee, you shouldn't have said that." The sad fact is, people don't want to know the truth. They don't want to hear bad news, or have their illusions tampered with. That's why when the My Lai massacre story first broke, people were angry at the reporter who broke it. The fact is, I was a lot easier on Mantle in *Ball Four* than the press ever realized. While putting the knock on the book a lot of sports writers made Mantle look worse than I ever intended, possibly because they were extrapolating their own experiences with him.

Everybody talks about what Mantle did for the game. Phil Linz did more. All Mantle really did for the game was become a great player and hit a lot of home runs. I think he did those things not for the game, but for himself. The kind of thing you do for the game is sign autographs, and show up at places you're not paid to show up at. What you do for the game is talk to reporters and be nice to the sweaty people outside the ball park. Muhammad Ali was good for boxing not only because he was a good fighter.

Still, I wouldn't want anybody to go away with

the feeling that I don't really like Mantle. In many ways he's had a difficult time of it. He was a moody guy and I suppose he was in pain a lot. I guess he was scared a lot, too, about people taking him and being dishonest with him. He had a lot of financial disasters and seemed to have a knack for trusting the wrong people (and mistrusting people he would have been better off trusting). But I'm not sure it's necessary to make excuses for him. On reflection, I suppose what I'll probably remember most about him is his sense of humor—even about the book. The only thing he ever said when asked what he thought of Jim Bouton's epic was, "Jim who?"

There's a song written by David Frishberg that appears in an album called "Oklahoma Toad." The title of the song is "Van Lingle Mungo." The words are, basically, just the names of ballplayers out of Frishberg's childhood and they're sung one after the other in a kind of lilting refrain: Whitey Kurowski, Johnny Sain, Eddie Joost, Johnny Pesky, Ferris Fain, Van Lingle Mungo. It's a very pleasant song, sad and haunting. Here is a man reliving his childhood through the names of old baseball players, men he admired and respected, maybe loved. For the first time, listening to that song, I had some twinges of regret about *Ball Four*. I felt that perhaps a kid reading it would be so turned off to baseball heroes that he would never want to write songs about them when he grew up, that he would never feel nostalgic about them. I wondered if I had really smashed heroes, whether I had ruined the game for the kids and ruined it for baseball fans.

Well, I thought about it, and then I thought about it some more. And I decided, no, that's not the way things work. I went through the same stage when I was a kid. I loved the Giants. I loved Alvin Dark and Dusty Rhodes and Sal Maglie. Even now, thinking back, I can remember exactly how I felt about these men. There is still that same rush of good feeling when I think about them and what they meant to me. Sal Maglie, the Barber, the old heavy-bearded master who used to go in and brush back the Dodgers with the curveball, the clever old competitor, the tough old guy who really put it to them. And Alvin "Blackie" Dark. I wonder how many people remember he was called Blackie; the clutch hitter with the black bat who worked those great double plays with Eddie Stanky. They're still the old Giants to me and my memories of them are still so happy that if I could write songs I'd write one about them.

But I think there are two Sal Maglies, two Alvin Darks, two Dusty Rhodes. There's the Dusty Rhodes who won a World Series pinch-hitting and the Dusty Rhodes who drove a bus in the World's Fair. I could write a song about one of them. But I'm writing no songs about the Alvin Dark who ignores kids who want his autograph.

And I'll write no songs about Sal Maglie, the pitching coach, *my* pitching coach, who did me more harm than good.

So I think it's possible that you can view people as heroes and at the same time understand that they are people, too, imperfect, narrow sometimes, even not very good at what they do. I didn't smash any heroes or ruin the game for anybody. You want heroes, you can have them. Heroes exist only in the mind anyway. David Frishberg has his heroes. I have mine. I just wish I could write songs.

6.

THE SUBJECT IS ROSES— AND DAFFODILS

I would hate anybody to think that my world turned narrow, bleak and argumentative because of *Ball Four*. The fact is that I had a marvelous time. The book didn't merely get me a new career in television, it opened a world, several worlds. Just writing it increased my perceptions. Suddenly I was not only laughing at funny things people said, I was remembering what was so funny. My ear got better, my eye sharper. Riding by a used-car lot in St. Louis, for example, I noticed that cars weren't being called "used" anymore. They were being called "preowned." Yes they were. And we all know that our kids say funny/ great things, only we can never remember what they were. Well, I remember. (I write them down.) Like my five-year-old daughter Laurie once called Astro Turf "pretend grass." I predict a great future for her.

Plus, the book made me famous, or at least notorious, and as a result there were some marvelous confrontations. One of them was with a trio of Baseball Annies who read me out one night near the bullpen in Montreal. "You Jim Bouton?" one of them said. I admitted it, bashfully. "We want to talk to you about your book."

I'll talk to *anyone* about my book.

It turned out they felt I had treated them, admitted Baseball Annies all three (and not too bad-looking), unfairly.

"We don't like the implications that anybody who is not a stewardess can't be class stuff," one said.

"We sleep with ballplayers," the second said. "What's the matter with us? I'm a teacher, she's a secretary, and she's a doctor. Do we look like sad creatures?"

"Wouldn't you consider us class stuff?" the third said.

And I said, "Ladies, I will give you every opportunity to prove yourselves."

I got to meet some famous people, and many of them were terrifically nice to me. Frank Gilroy, who wrote *The Subject Was Roses*, stopped me in the Chicago airport and said he loved the book. "You know, I used to be bored when the relief pitchers started to come in to the ballgame. But after reading your book, I find myself wondering what they're thinking. I wonder if he's saying to himself, 'Why are they using me in this situation? Don't they think much of me?' Or maybe he's thinking, 'One more good outing. I need another good outing to stay in the big leagues.'

You know, you gave me a lot of insight into the game that I never had before. And as a result I get a much bigger kick out of it."

Thank you, Frank Gilroy.

I also met The Sensuous Woman. We were both plugging our books in Los Angeles. She (her name is Terry Garrity) said, would you believe, that most of the interviewers she talked to praised her book before and after the show and even during the commercials. During the show, they tore it up. Imagine that.

Since we were both free that evening, I invited her to dinner and we caught Mel Tormé at the Century Plaza. Nothing came of it, though, possibly because I hadn't brought along any Reddi-Whip. Still, I'm fond of the lady. I spent seventeen weeks under *The Sensuous Woman* on the *Times* best-seller list. That builds something.

I got kissed by Morgana. She's a stripper who got herself a lot of publicity by dashing onto baseball fields during games and kissing somebody—player, umpire, batboy, whoever was available. So she was invited on the Merv Griffin show at the same time I was. (A lot of TV producers think like that.) That's how I got kissed by Morgana. She may have breasts the size of watermelons and as soft as strawberry Jell-O, but boy, are her lips greasy.

Anyway, she showed up in Los Angeles one evening while the Astro pitchers were running in the outfield. She came bouncing bra-less down the aisle, and for some reason several Astro pitchers said to Coach Jim Owens, "Hey Jim, how about a little break? A little break, please."

"No breaks," Owens said sternly. Then he turned around and caught a glimpse of Morgana. "Oh Jesus," he said. "Yeah. Everybody rest a minute."

We rested. And we ogled Morgana and she ogled back. Jim Owens forgot how many sprints we had run. He said, "Ah, forget it." Jim Owens is a great pitching coach.

And one time at a party I ran into Larry Ritter, who wrote *The Glory of Their Times*, that marvelous book of recollections of old baseball players. He stuck out his hand and said, "Nice to meet you. I think you wrote the second greatest baseball book of all time."

There was, in addition, all that appearing on television. I was never exactly allergic to television and there I was, hitting all the big ones. I was on so many of those talk shows I worked out a rating system. The worst was Johnny Carson. I didn't go on his show because, he said, I didn't go on it first. That earned him a very low spot in my poll.

Then Merv Griffin. He nailed down his spot by saying to me, five minutes before air time, "Listen, I haven't read your book. What would you like me to ask you?" Drove me right up the wall.

After that came Dick Cavett. I'd heard he was great about reading books of the authors who came on his show and I was prepared for a good, in-depth interview. Instead I got a very superficial few minutes during which it became painfully plain that Cavett hadn't done his homework either.

I don't think David Frost read the book. On the other hand, he got a good briefing from his competent young producer who had read it. As a result Frost managed to ask just the right questions, put me at my ease and establish the kind of rapport that brought out the best in me. If that's what he intended, and I'm sure he did, he did a lovely job.

The best TV man of all only has a radio show. He is Studs Terkel, the Chicago broadcaster and author of *Hard Times*. Not only had he read the book, and thoroughly, making a lot of notes which he distributed through the leaves of his copy, he showed enormous and incisive comprehension. He started the show with a taped selection from *The Glory of Their Times* in which one of the old players talked about the kinds of things that went on in his day, and they turned out, of course, to be not so different than the things I wrote about in *Ball Four*. We went on from there. A good, intelligent job.

A lot of other nice things happened.

Like I got a call, two calls, for goodness' sakes, in *Oh! Calcutta!* During the first act all these naked people are talking about how one of the guys has a problem that Masters and Johnson would no doubt call premature ejaculation. And one of the actors said, "If you think he comes quick, wait'll you meet Jim Bouton. He comes if you just look at him." I nearly fell off my seat. My wife had the good grace to laugh.

And later on, while an actress was front and center naked, one of the actors said, "Hey Jim, how would you like to ball four that?"

Now that's what I call *fame*. I mean, *Penthouse* asked me to model raincoats and I modeled bathing suits for *Esquire*. And the Encyclopedia Britannica collected my biography. You don't get that even for winning twenty.

At the beginning I was very anxious to find out the reactions of the guys on the other clubs, especially the Milwaukee club, about which most of *Ball Four* was written. (It was the Seattle Pilots then.) Steve Hovley was my man there. This is one of his reports:

> The ball club is really in an uproar. Every guy on the club has a copy of the magazine and the excerpt is the topic of conversation from the time the bus leaves the hotel until the bus returns from the ball park after the game. They're all looking at the dates in there and trying to figure out how many other dates are going to be in the book and what they might have done on them. John

O'Donoghue was insisting that you would have to use "bleep" in the book. I assured him, however, that the real words were being used throughout. Another subject for debate was whether it would be a long book or a short book and I told them 400 pages. They went out of their minds.

I've been debating with a lot of guys about the book. Well, not actually debating. I just throw a morsel of thought on the waters and they thrash and snatch after it. They're very emotional. Gene Brabander wants to know how you'd like to take a ball in the chest.

The first day we got to the park after the excerpt came out, Dave Bristol [the manager] said, "This won't affect my judgment of you as ballplayers and I don't want it to affect your play. But I do wish you wouldn't take those greenies." Then he went into a stock ten-minute dissertation on why greenies are bad for you. During the meeting O'Donoghue was sitting in front of his locker with his head in his hands.

"And I didn't even get those greenies for myself," he said. "I don't take them, I swear. I just got them for the other guys. And I'm the guy who gets into the book." Poor John.

And Skip Lockwood said, "There's one good thing about the book being 400 pages long—a lot of them won't be finished with it by the time the summer is over."

Jim Colborn, pitcher and Chicago Cub player rep, was called upon to comment on *Ball Four* on television one morning. First there was a filmed interview with Joe Pepitone, who said the book was very bad for the game. (It might also have been the time he was asked to what he attributed the success of the book and his answer was, "Every time I rip it, they sell fifty more copies. I'm not going to rip it anymore.") At any rate, Colborn went on camera and said that he liked the book, especially because he identified with me and recognized the truths. "I highly recommend it to everyone," he said. He also said he had a deal with Bouton that if he didn't like the book, Bouton would refund the purchase price. "I'm not going to ask for it," Colborn said.

The day I got to Oklahoma City after being sent down from Houston, the visiting team in town was Indianapolis. Dooley Womack, a man I kidded a bit in *Ball Four* ("You mean I got traded for Dooley Womack? *The* Dooley Womack?"), was on that club. He'd been taking a lot of kidding and wasn't very happy about it. When he saw me he ducked away, mumbling, "Fuck 'im, fuck 'im."

Kurt Bevacqua, an Indianapolis rookie, came over and said he loved the book, and the parts about Dooley were the funniest. Possibly as payment for all the joy I had given him, Bevacqua got the last organized baseball hit off J. Bouton, a home run. I mentioned that earlier, didn't I? Well, it's important—at least, to me and Bevacqua.

Sande Padwe of the Philadelphia *Inquirer* tells me that copyboys there are playing a game based on *Ball Four*. The game is called "Who Said That?" The way it's played somebody says, "Who said, 'Hiya blondie, how's your old tomato?' " The first one to say Joe Schultz scores a point.

That's almost as good as being mentioned in a crossword puzzle.

At a restaurant in St. Louis three young women at a table stopped me as I was walking by. They said I was spoiling all their fun, that a lot of wives had taken to traveling with their husbands. A lot of girls have told me that. What was funny about this encounter was that at one point, after we were seated at a nearby table, I dropped my fork. When I bent down to pick it up, one of the girls shouted at me, "What are you trying to do, Bouton, get a beaver shot?"

Some of the guys tried to help me out when they knew I was feeling low—like just before I went in to see the Commissioner. "You know something?" Jack DiLauro said, "I'm pissed off at your book too."

"You too, Jack?"

"Yeah, you son of a bitch. You didn't have me in it."

And I was running in the outfield before that terrible game in Shea Stadium and Tom Griffin began to run alongside me. "Hey Leper, how do you feel?" he said.

"Pretty down."

"Look," he said, "if you think you did the right thing, well, give it time. It'll blow over."

There are times when a kind word is a rare treasure.

Not long after I was out of baseball I got a call from a guy in New Jersey who wanted to know if I would be willing to lend my name and presence to a basketball team which would tour the country. The team would be called Jim Bouton and the U.S. Beavers. I said no, thanks.

This one appeared in *Sports Illustrated:* Andy Armour, eleven-year-old baseball fan, to a friend to whom he had just loaned a copy of Jim Bouton's *Ball Four:* "If you run across any words you don't understand, whatever you do don't ask your mother to explain them."

At bottom I don't understand all the fuss created by revelations that baseball players take greenies, otherwise known as amphetamines, or ups. In fact, Larry Dierker and I have decided that what baseball needs is an even better pill —a large, all-purpose pill; maybe not just baseball, perhaps all sports. We could, we decided, call it a Sports Pill. This pill should contain Darvon (pain-killer) for your arm (or whatever else hurts), aspirin for headache, greenies to clear up hangovers (incipient and otherwise) and tetracycline to ward off the clap. Dierker and I figured a pill like that would make us millionaires in a matter of months.

Despite all the denials from Elston Howard that he used to doctor up the ball for Whitey Ford (or that Whitey *liked* to throw a baseball that was artfully maimed), Yogi Berra himself told this story. At a recent old-timers' game, Ford, who claimed a record of about 0–5 in exhibitions of that sort, scuffed up a ball that he threw to Dom DiMaggio. The ball dropped about a foot. Later, Ford explained to Berra in the dugout, "I'm tired of losing in old-timers' games."

The *Sporting News* is what is called the bible of baseball. I'd always considered it conservative and basically representative of the point of view of the baseball hierarchy. So when C. C. Johnson Spink, the publisher, asked me to stop by his office for a chat, I was rather nervous about it. To my surprise, C.C. said he loved the book. He also said that he'd like to see more of that kind of baseball reporting. "I've tried to do something about the pap some contributors send me [for the *Sporting News*], but it's been an uphill struggle."

And then his managing editor, Lowell Reidenbaugh, wrote a long, very favorable article about me and *Ball Four*. Take that, Commissioner.

Did anybody notice that Carl Yastrzemski picked up rapidly as a player in about June of 1970 and wound up having an extraordinary season? Well, several Boston fans have written to say that it was because I wrote that Yaz had a bit of dog in him. They said it woke him up like Pavlov's bell. They thanked me. They might be right. The year Eddie Stanky called Yaz an "All Star from the neck down," Yastrzemski won the Triple Crown and Boston won the pennant.

George Culver, Houston pitcher, tells me that there is nothing worse than a panty-hose beaver. I rather agree.

I sat near Johnny Bench at the Washington Baseball Writers' Dinner and he said, "I read where you said Pete Rose and I got on you from the dugout worse than anybody. Well, I want you to know we really weren't that upset about the book. Pete and I got on everybody. So don't worry about it."

Who's worried? I do want to point out something, though. Pete Rose wrote a book last year too. It was his autobiography. He said it was the first book he ever read. He said he liked it.

While in Washington I took the opportunity to have a chat with Phil Hollywood, who is manager of the Shoreham Hotel, the beaver-shooting capitol of the world. He said he and most of the other employees of the hotel had read *Ball Four* with great relish. Hollywood said he'd worked at the Shoreham for twenty-five years and even in his earliest days he remembered getting complaints that there were people running around on the roof. "Right away I'd think, 'Which ball club is in town?'" Hollywood said. "Actually I didn't mind that they were up there. I was just afraid that someone would fall off."

You know, I've wondered about that myself. There's no railing up there and there are overwhelming reasons to lean out. I guess heaven protects the daring beaver shooter.

Now a roster of comments * about the book that amused me.

Eddie O'Brien. I gave him hell in *Ball Four*. He was only in baseball—as a coach—to pick up some extra pension money. Anyway, this is something he said to Bill Schonely, the Seattle broad-

---

* Most of the quotes were gathered by my private investigating force of John Leptich of Chicago and Marc Risman of Beverly Hills.

caster: "When you see Bouton, tell him I didn't say hello."

Paul Richards, Atlanta general manager: "If there's anything in that book about me, I'll sue." Well, there was something. He's quoted in it as calling Marvin Miller, our Marvin Miller, a mustachioed four-flusher. He didn't sue. Not only that, he once told a man he thought was his friend: "The thing that burns me up the most about that damn book is that we have to sell it in our own ball park."

Jimmy Ray of the Astros: "If the Commissioner cuts off greenies because of your goddam book, I personally will snipe your ass."

Julian Javier of the St. Louis Cardinals: "At least he didn't pick on the little guys."

Dave Nelson, Washington infielder: "Hilarious but true. I'm not a big name so no one will quote me."

Rudy May, Angel pitcher: "It's all true. That's the chilling part of it."

Mary Jane Johnstone, wife of Jay Johnstone, former Angel outfielder: "It was great. Other players are afraid to have the book in their house because their wives might read it."

William Feeney, fifteen, son of Chub Feeney, president of the National League, to his father: "Dad, it's really a great book."

Juan Marichal, Giant pitcher: "If it's the truth, no matter how bad it is, I have to go along with it."

Willie Mays: "I don't read them kind of books."

Tony Kubek of NBC: "A lot of lies."

Dick Williams, manager, Oakland: "I didn't read it. I didn't like it. I don't think he had any business writing it."

Junior Gilliam, coach, Los Angeles: "If most of the players don't like it, I don't like it."

Joe Schultz, former manager of the Seattle Pilots: "What the shit. The more I think about it, it's not so bad."

Some day there'll be a movie made of *Ball Four*. Only Joe Schultz could play Joe Schultz.

7.

ADVERTISEMENTS
FOR MYSELF

The line is Norman Mailer's, of course. And I should be too modest to use it, right? Like I got a lot to be modest about, right? Right, right. On the other hand, I tell myself, who else is going to enshrine the best reviews of *Ball Four* between hard covers? It turns out, nobody. Not even me.

My impulse was to run them from top to bottom, beginning to end, every delicious goddam comma. I'll tell you why I wanted so much to do it. From the time the excerpts of *Ball Four* first appeared in *Look* until the book showed up in stores, and even for a time thereafter, I took, as I've explained, a lot of abuse in a lot of places. During that time, biting on a bullet, I said, just wait, you bastards, just wait until the guys who read books for a living come in with their reviews. They'll understand and they'll make you guys look like, well, like the bunch of frustrated things you are. Sometimes I even believed it.

Yet that's the way it happened. It was like having an elaborate daydream and then watching it work out in real life in every respect. Eerie. It reached the point where, like Muhammad Ali at his best, I could shout, whee, me!

So I honestly wanted to enshrine these reviews. Except too many people, many of whom I trusted, told me it would be a bit much. They warned I could ruin my shoulder patting myself on the back, that instead of turning people on, I would turn them off. It would be, they said, like an over-the-hill ham actor, sitting around reading his old notices out loud. Still, I was not altogether convinced that the whole world wouldn't be as happy to sit around reading my notices as I am. There must be millions of people, I reasoned, who didn't get to read them first time around.

In the end, though, I was convinced, sort of. So all you unfortunates are going to get here are highlights—the best reviews (in my opinion) and why I loved them.

If I had to pick a personal favorite it would be George Frazier's in the Boston *Globe*. Frazier is not strictly a book reviewer, of course. He is a columnist. It's important, though, that he is not a sports columnist. I particularly liked two things in Frazier's column. One had to do with his opinion that

> It is a document for these days of dedication to changing the older order. Modestly and ingratiatingly, it is an authentic revolutionary manifesto.

Me and Che Guevara.

The other involved Frazier's picking up on Joe Cronin, president of the American League, making a clumsy attempt to influence Marvin Miller.

> Joe Cronin. The arrogance of ignorance . . . Who the hell does Joe Cronin think he is, trying to bully Marvin Miller around? Joe Cronin, who fired umpire Bill Valentine for alleged incompetence. It is one of the consumer services of *Ball Four* that it points out that Valentine was perhaps the only umpire who dared call Mickey Mantle out on borderline pitches. Joe Cronin! Doesn't Joe Cronin realize that we now live in a new time, a time when he is an anachronism, an enemy of those who provide us with pleasure in the summer of the year by playing a boys' game with incomparable grace?

Then Bob Lipsyte of *The New York Times*. His review was not his first column on *Ball Four*. He wrote the first one off the articles in *Look* and, as I said earlier, helped save my sanity after that terrible Memorial Day weekend. I'm told there are people who only buy the *Times* on Mondays, Thursdays and Saturdays, the days Lipsyte's column appears. I can understand why. Anyway, here are some of the things he said in his review column.

The excerpts contained much of the top, sensational aspects of the book. . . . In the context of the book . . . this aspect reappears sympathetically as a natural outgrowth of a game in which 25 young, insecure, undereducated men of narrow skills keep circling the country to play before fans who do not understand their problems or their work, and who use them as symbols for their own fantasies.

In return, the players have a certain contempt for the fans, abusing the camp followers . . . and refusing to sign autographs for the kids.

For the players are truly dependent on each other for moral support and appreciation and technical help . . . because [the player] is family and the other side of the fence is thick with rubes. . . .

Whether one considers Bouton a bringer of truth or a tattletale, there is probably no point following baseball this year unless you read the book.

Pete Axthelm is sports editor of *Newsweek*. Actually, he jumped the gun on the publication date of *Ball Four*. This means he came out cool right smack in the middle of all the heat. It came as no surprise to this writer. Axthelm has a knack for showing up in the middle of a lot of heat.

And no one has yet knocked him out of the kitchen. Most important, he hit the nail on the head first off:

> Basically, *Ball Four* is meant to be fun, but it touches on some important issues. . . . Such candid observations may well hasten Bouton's departure from baseball, and some of his critics may assume he couldn't care less. But the emotion that flows through *Ball Four* makes it clear that the author really does believe in his imperfect, often silly sport.

David Halberstam is one of the young, tough reporters who told the world what was really going on in Vietnam before anybody wanted to know. He won a Pulitzer Prize for doing it. That was when he worked for *The New York Times*. Then he went to *Harper's* for a while. The piece he did there on *Ball Four* was less a review than a commentary on the journalism of our times.

> He has written . . . a book deep in the American vein, so deep in fact that it is by no means a sports book . . . a comparable insider's book about, say, the Congress of the United States, the Ford Motor Company, or the Joint Chiefs of Staff would be equally welcome. . . .

As the book is deeply in the American

vein, so is the reaction against it. The sportswriters are not judging the accuracy of the book, but Bouton's right to tell (that is, your right to read), which is, again, as American as apple pie or the White House press corps. A reporter covers an institution, becomes associated with it, protective of it, and, most important, the arbiter of what is right to tell. He knows what's good for you to hear, what should remain at the press-club bar. When someone goes beyond that, stakes out a new dimension of what is proper and significant, then it is not the ballplayers who yell the most, nor in Washington the public-information officers, but indeed the sportswriters or the Washington bureau chiefs, because having played the game, having been tamed, when someone outflanks them, they must of necessity attack his intentions, his accuracy. Thus Bouton has become a social leper to many sportswriters and thus Sy Hersh, when he broke the My Lai story, became a "peddler" to some of Washington's most famous journalists.

Then there was the review in the daily *Times*. A lot of books don't get reviewed there. Some are panned. Few sports books are so well reviewed. I was awed, especially by these lines, written by Christopher Lehmann-Haupt:

Jim Bouton has actually gotten me interested in baseball again, and I didn't think
that was possible. . . . *Ball Four* is a people
book, not just a baseball book.

You know, when the book was nearly done I
had begun to think that. You can't imagine the
joy I got when somebody like Lehmann-Haupt
noticed.

One could have a brain of stone (I've often been
accused of just that), and still be affected by people who tell you that you have ruined the youth
of America. So it was still nice to read the review
by a priest, George G. Hill, in *The Christian
Century.* I was impressed that he made no mention of some of the language used. I guess he was
not offended.

Erich Fromm has said that more than
theology we need a science of "idology." He
sees hope for more human unity and for human betterment in idology: people can agree
more readily about what God is *not* than
about what or who he *is;* life will be better
if people will recognize their idols as idols
and quit worshiping them. Jim Bouton's book
. . . makes a contribution to the needed dei-
dolizing of the American Way of Life by
desacralizing one of its holy symbols. . . .

Except for baseball itself, the most per-
sistent theme throughout the book is "beaver

shooting" . . . pursued ingeniously with the help of hotel roofs, telescopes . . . closets in hotel rooms, and (a delightful touch) places to look up under the stands while the national anthem is being played. . . .

Read it. It constitutes a positive contribution to the needed moral reordering of America—and it's a lot of fun.

See, I've been trying to say that beaver shooting is *respectable*. Now I have an important and respectable ally.

There were several things that Wilfrid Sheed said in *Life* that warmed my cockles. I like having my cockles warmed. He understood, for example, that in almost any other business, a *Ball Four* would not be shocking at all. ("The people he names by name are probably secretly proud to be in there.") Then there was this:

The real problem is the game's missionary complex, dating back to the days when ballplayers couldn't eat in decent restaurants and were considered slightly scurvier than actors. If anyone from that era had been told baseball and organized labor would be the last strongholds of bourgeois respectability, he'd have bust his watchchain laughing. But that's how it goes with moral revolutions.

And this:

> For all the pious whinnies over Bouton's
> book, the baseball establishment can prob-
> ably stand having the players exposed—in
> fact it may even be good for business: top-
> dollar adults were getting awfully tired of
> the short-haired, cliché-bearing prigs we used
> to get. . . .

And this, which sort of put me away:

> His book is not only the best and funniest
> account I know of that strange gypsy cara-
> van known as a ball team and its trackless
> wanderings . . . but a serious moral investi-
> gation of a profession, a cousin of *From
> Here to Eternity*, though without the mur-
> derous bitterness of most such investigations.

Today James Jones. Tomorrow the world.

Finally there was Roger Angell in *The New
Yorker*. It's the dream of nearly every writer, I
am told, to get a favorable review in this extraor-
dinarily well-edited if sometimes snobbish magazine. That's not why I was so moved to get the
good review for *Ball Four* there. What moved me
is that it was written by Angell. You have only
to read his too-infrequent pieces on baseball to
realize the depth of his love for the game of baseball. Angell *knows* the game, understands it, rec-

ognizes the nuances, even likes the people in it, most of them anyway. And there I was, the Great Destroyer of the game. If I really was, Angell would have hated me.

Among the kind of things Angell wrote:

> The success here is Mr. Bouton himself as a day-to-day observer, hard thinker, marvellous listener, comical critic, angry victim, and unabashed lover of a sport . . . What he has given us . . . is a rare view of a highly complex public profession seen from the innermost side, along with an ironic and courageous mind. And, very likely, the funniest book of the year.

Of course, I'm lucky. I can keep those reviews handy—in all their delicious totality. Often, I just sit around reading and grooving.

It has never been told in detail exactly how *Ball Four* came to be written. Bouton knows, but modesty forbids him to tell precisely how things began. That's because it was with an act of generosity—Jim Bouton's, that is. So I'll tell it.

Winter, 1968. I had left the New York *Post*, where I was a columnist, some years before in order to go free-lance. I knew Bouton rather well —that is, better than I knew a great many of the other Yankees. I knew him better for two reasons. One was that he was more interesting and more fun to talk to than others. The other was that when I covered the Yankees, I was bemused by his fan club and the newspaper it put out called "All About Bouton." I had written all about the club, all about the paper and all about Bouton several times and as a result was invited to the annual Jim Bouton Fan Club Dinner, thrown, as I recall, in a little restaurant in the wilds of Queens (or was it The Bronx?). In the days when I was covering baseball, that was getting fairly close with a player, especially for a reporter who was not exactly a club favorite (on the ground that the club was never sure how much truth he was going to tell).

It was in that winter of 1968 that I was asked by a television station to prepare an interview as an audition. Through the years I have been asked to do this by several stations, although I have never, as a result, been offered a job as a sports newscaster. I don't think the world of television is exactly ready for the curious, chubby visage of L. Shecter. Nor do I believe I audition very well. And I'm not so sure that I *want* to be a television newscaster, although there are many pressures to do the auditions anyway. Ah, the pressures.

Casting about for a likely interviewee, I hit upon J. Bouton. There were several reasons. He had relatively recently returned from Mexico City where, during the Olympics, he had acted for the American Committee on Africa in proselytizing athletes to move against the future admission of South Africa to the Games. He would, as a result, make an interesting, timely interview. Another factor was that because of some kind of union or manpower problem or both, the interview would have to take place on a cold, windswept corner at eight o'clock in the morning. No matter how friendly you are with anybody, much less a relatively famous athlete, it is a great imposition to ask him to drive into New York from his suburban home at an ungodly hour of the morning to do a street interview that almost certainly would never get on television. Jim Bouton never hesitated. "What time?" he said. And he was there, on time.

The interview went rather well, I thought. (So well that a year later I was called back for another audition by the same station. I didn't get a job offer after that one, either.) Afterward, cold, sleepy, Bouton and I had breakfast at a nearby restaurant. It was over the bacon and eggs (I think) that he told me about the Korean boy he had recently adopted. As any free-lance writer will tell you, people are never simply people to him. They are always possible subjects for magazine articles. It struck me immediately that the story of a baseball player and his interracial adoption should make an interesting magazine article. The more Bouton talked about it, the more he recounted funny, touching incidents, the more certain I became that I was right.

I asked him if he would cooperate if I could find a magazine interested in such an article, and Bouton said what he always said in such circumstances: "Of course."

I wrote a brief outline, sent it off to my agent, and forgot about it. Amazing how many editors (including those at Look) didn't want to buy such a sweet story of a minor league baseball player and his adoption. After some months the story, or at least the outline, was sold to a travel magazine called *Signature,* the propaganda arm of the Diner's Club. It is not one of the best-paying magazines in America, but free-lancers can seldom be terribly selective.

I was in the shower that morning, preparing to go out to Bouton's home with a photographer, when I began to think about another project. (The free-lance mind at work.) I had recently read *Instant Replay,* which was written by Jerry Kramer of Green Bay and edited by Dick Schaap. It was a good book and I was impressed with its popularity. In the shower, where I do some of my best concentrated thinking (you can't, after all, read a newspaper in the shower), it occurred to me that perhaps the world was now ready for a baseball diary; not a *Dick Merriwell Wins His Spikes* which, I'm afraid, I considered the level of most baseball book writing, but a down-to-earth, honest-to-goodness report of the day-to-day activities of a real, live, sweaty baseball player.

I had not had much experience working closely with other people on writing projects. Back in the dim past I had tried to collaborate with a New York assistant DA who had helped put Frankie Carbo in jail. We had several long sessions, I wrote the piece and showed it to the DA. "Why, I can't say that," he spluttered.

"You *did* say it."

"Yes, but I didn't realize how it would look in print."

Well, we pulled and tugged and doctored and rewrote and in the end the article wasn't worth much. This was easily detected by the magazine editor and it was never published. It was then I made my vow—no more collaborations, no more editing other people's lives, no more hard work down the drain because somebody chickened out.

When I thought of Bouton, however, these objections no longer seemed especially valid. If Bouton agreed to do a diary, I decided, he would do an honest one and not back off when he saw it in print. I've been wrong about a lot of things in my life, but not that.

At Bouton's home that day I asked him if he would be interested in doing such a diary. As I wrote in the Foreword to *Ball Four*, he said, "Funny you should mention that. I've been keeping notes."

I should also point out that Bouton had just spent a season, and a mediocre one at that, with Seattle, a minor league team. He was now going to start out with the same club, now an expansion major league team. That is, he was going to spring training with it. There was no guarantee he would make the club. He was, in fact, sent down to Vancouver, a farm team, early in the season. When that happened, we had no way of knowing whether he'd *ever* return to the major leagues. I don't think it would have mattered. What we had going for us was Bouton, and he takes himself along wherever he goes.   L.S.

8

SWEET AND
SOUR MASH NOTES

The mail on *Ball Four*, both on the condensation in *Look* and the book itself (although not, at this writing, counting the paperback), was so heavy that it was almost impossible to keep track. Thus I can only say I got 1,247 letters. Of these 1,213 were positive, 34 negative. But who's counting?

I will not burden the world with detailed reports of the people who wrote to tell me how much they agree/love/sympathize with me. However, there were some letters that were, at least to me, especially amusing/touching/understanding/cogent. They follow.* (Most have been edited for length.)

* I should explain about letters and the law. Letters belong to the people who write them. Just because somebody writes you a letter, it doesn't mean you can do with it what you please. You can't, for one thing, publish it, at least without permission. In some cases, especially those in which the identity of the writer is important, this permission has been obtained. In other cases, where permission wasn't solicited or was refused, the name and address of the writer have been disguised. These signatures bear an asterisk.

From the time I was 19 until last year (a span of about five years), I went out with baseball players. I never "went through an entire team" or anything as seamy as that—I just considered that I had good relationships with a select few people, sometimes platonically. And, I always said (along with my roommates who also dated them) that I would've loved to write a book about the whole situation. . . . I know that many players feel hostile about anyone telling what goes on after they leave the field but it really is about time that someone knocked them off their pedestals and revealed the truth (that they're not heroes off of Wheatie boxes but just men—horny men at that!).

Sincerely,
Sarah Andreas*
Cleveland, Ohio

P.S. George Brunet DOES SO wear underwear

(The following was inscribed on the flyleaf of a book titled *Blue Movie*.)

From one fantastic dead-eye beaver man to another, with greatest admiration and all best wishes.

Terry Southern

If you ever want to write a book about the "athlete in bed" I have some blond divorcee friends who have fractured me with tales of their "dates" with Baseball players—Hockey players etc! . . . For instance Mayo Smith admits losing his virginity to a sun-warmed watermelon his dad had just plugged.

> Hang in there darlin!
> Alice Freese*
> *Nashville, Tenn.*

I was the spring training batboy for the Pittsburgh Pirates. . . . My earliest recollections of that gang include a guy named Stan Rojek. . . . Rojek would split a bat, then pry it between the old wood boards (in the dugout) eventually spreading and warping the boards, generally affording Rojek and the others a grand view of a blonde's crotch. . . . My other vivid memory was of an outfielder named Wally Westlake. I was 14-years old at the time . . . and my first day on the job as batboy Westlake kneeled next to me. "You live around here?" questioned Wally. I acknowledged I did. "Then," he asked, "where's the whorehouse?"

> Most Cordially,
> Bennett J. Mintz
> *Sherman Oaks, Cal.*

It's a gasser and reminds me of the days I was playing, and I was in that same Tacoma dressing room 22–23 years ago!! It was just as bad then, in the old Western International League. . . . We had some real "beavers" too, especially with Lefty O'Doul's old San Francisco Seals. Brucie Ogrodamski, a catcher, who has since died, led the midnight corps of voyeurs. He had all the tricks including the brace and bit, and "over-the-transom" spyglasses.

Best regards,
James F. Bryan*
Chicago, Ill.

I last attended a major league baseball game in Washington in the summer of 1934. It was the only one I ever got to; it wasn't very interesting so I didn't go back. But I have read your book which is excellent. And since I've tried the same art form I'm something of an expert. I know how easy it is to decide nothing happened on this day —or dismiss the day with a perfunctory line.

I'm writing this in England but I'm asking my secretary in Cambridge to send you a copy of my imitation of Pepys. It's a small return for the pleasure you've given me.

Yours faithfully,
John Kenneth Galbraith
Cambridge, Mass.

We are rudely disturbed by the way you critizied many ball players espiecilly *Joe Pepitone*, Mickey Mantle, Elston Howard, ect. We have read that one day Pepi shook off a pick-off sign,

172

maybe he was afraid you could not reach first base. My friends and I think you are a disgrace to the Houston Astros one of the finest teams in the National Leage. . . . IF YOU WOULD LEAVE! I am writing a letter to Manager Harry Walker to express my opionion like thousands of others that dislike you.

In my opion you are a horny, sexual——!!!

Sincerely,
Mr. Samuel Luigi*
& friends
Bronx, N.Y.

P.S. Confucious say: He who takes off all his clothes is like horny old Kraphead Bouton!!!

"BRAVO" E Fornicateium—Latin for those who don't understand. One request: If movie is contemplated, please let Jim Pagliaroni play Jim Pagliaroni. I feel qualified in saying that I could play the part of a Deranged, Perverted, Iconoclastic, Moral Degenerate, Loving Father, Loving Husband and above all a Majestic Hypocrit, with tremendous gusto.

Luv,
Pag.
Grass Valley, Cal.

I did a book report on [Ball Four] in high school and got a C-. (Only because the teacher was a fan of Mantle and he thought your book was just a bunch of lies just so you could make some cheap money.) I did not pay any attention.

Best of luck
your friend,
Tom Paradise
Hicksville, N.Y.

I've always *loathed* baseball—I've *always* associated the game with morons on either side of the stands. Despite the fact that my *husband* knows every statistic since Doubleday invented the damn game. So help me, he has a statistic book which he reads like a bible, sitting on the John, would you believe! . . . I swear, since reading your book Ball Four, I have begun to read the *baseball* page, with interest! I even told my husband I wouldn't mind attending a game (he nearly drove off the road at *that* suggestion!).

Buona Fortuna—always!
Elizabeth Seideman
Scarsdale, N.Y.

We are two high school seniors who are avid baseball fans. . . . Both of us agree with your feelings about Fred Talbot, and we feel we should inform you of a game that we invented two years ago. It was a baseball-dice game where hitters and pitchers were rated according to their talents. We designed it so that the better hitters would have a better opportunity to get a hit. (For you to get a hit, we had to throw 3 "6's" with the three dice provided.)

The pitchers were also rated according to ability. In order to keep each game close we had a "FRED TALBOT" card. Any time one of us was leading by 10 or more runs, we were forced to bring in Talbot for 1 inning. Talbot's card had only one way to retire a batter; triple snake-eyes!

Sincerely,
Wes Wenk
John Marx
Highland Park, Ill.

I am at a loss to reconcile your reasoning in writing this rubbish. It is on a level with Mrs. Mead's published statement that marijuana is O.K. for teenagers, as it is no worse than alcohol. It serves no constructive purpose, only to tear down established values for the sake of destruction. You have done no service to the youth of America, believe me.

Ray Wieboldt
Westbury, N.Y.

I'am 14 years old and I just finished your book. I thought it was great! My Grandfather didn't like it very well.

Yeah surre.
Mike Lynch
Lake Oswego, Oregon

One last comment . . . and perhaps the one I feel strongest about is your viewpoint on the racial situation in professional baseball. A few years ago I was having a drink with a couple of friends on the Mets and I jokingly said, "How come you guys lost tonight?" Well, to my utter amazement the question was answered by ——— [sorry about that, folks] who said, "Because there are too many niggers on the team." I suppose you couldn't expect much from a Texan (perhaps my own little bit of prejudice) but it shocked me none the less. I found myself completely unaccepted by the majority of athletes I know (you may call me a Baseball Annie as you put it in your book, but most of them are simply platonic friends. . . . I'm a bit more choosy than Chicago Shirley) when it was learned that I was having an affair with a Negro athlete. . . . After I danced with him at the party the night before the Martin Luther King game, there were few white people there that talked to me.

trv*

Anaheim, Cal.

Hello Big Mouth. You got everybody reading that sh--a--book, but they're reading it. Get that money. Oh yes, I've been offered four movie contracts. Everybody, after reading your book, thinks I'm some kind of actor.

Tommy Davis

YOU ARE A NO GOOD LOUSY BASTARD.
Unsigned
Wilmette, Ill.

I've been connected with a sportswriting family all my life and that half of the family probably won't like your book—but so far my husband and I think it's great. . . . Thanks for having the courage. Not many people can go for that old fairy-tale world any more.

When all the big deals are screaming at you, remember—we care and we're for you. Can't sign my name—would be disinherited—

Best regards—
Us

(The following notes were written on a Christmas card by a couple whose marriage I was supposed to have destroyed in *Ball Four*.)

Just a line to let you know we think of you often, miss you and hope that you have a great fucking holiday season also.

Nan Gar & Babe [Bell]

P.S. All our love

Thanks to that fucking book of yours I can't get a job anywhere in baseball or out. We hope you have plenty of room because we're thinking of moving in with you. Drop us a line when you have time, ass eyes.

Our best
Nan & Gary [Bell]

(An anecdote about Ted Williams in *Ball Four* revealed that this great hitter used to psych himself up for a game during batting practice by screaming: "My name is Ted fucking Williams and I'm the greatest hitter in baseball." The following letter was sent, apparently, partly as a result of that anecdote.)

I was hitting .570 in American Legion. I kept telling myself I've been lucky and that I can't keep it up. So what happens. I am now hitting .375 after a terrible slump where, just as you said, I thought I would never get a hit. So from now on, when I get hot, I'm Jim fucking Kamler and I'm going to hit that little shit slider just like Ted Fucking Williams.

Sincerely,
Jim Kamler*
Los Angeles, Cal.

It's a shame that a national magazine has the space to publish the "junk" that rolls off the tongue of a loser!!

Yes, I mean loser—in the big game—life!!

Yours truly
"Bud" Kempton*

I want to congratulate you on your success with *Ball Four*. I bought it in Houston in July, and both Nolan [Ryan, N.Y. Mets] and I enjoyed it very much. We have often discussed the pretentiousness, the loneliness, and the frustrations which accompany baseball; and your honesty and subtle sense of humor captured that aspect so well.

Sincerely,
Ruth Ryan
Flushing, N.Y.

I confess that I was biased against your book before I read it. As a historian I should have gone to the book first, but regrettably let my prejudices prevent me from making an unbiased opinion. I am a counselor in a college, and believe in "confidential material." What people tell me in confidence I consider a sacred trust, and no one is to know of these intimate matters in people's lives. For this reason I thought it was "bush" for you to write about the intimate affairs of the clubhouse and bullpen, and create a best seller out of other people's lives. But, I was wrong, and I want to explain my change of heart!

For too long America has idolized its baseball

players as some kind of gods whose integrity and superhuman qualities must never be questioned. What your book did for me was to make me realize that baseball players . . . are subject to the same pressures, the same tensions, and problems that confront us all.

Dr. Richard Lyon Morgan
Professor of Psychology
Mitchell College
Statesville, N.C.

(The following was written in the margin of a newspaper clipping describing the arrival of a young pitcher named Dick Baney, "part of Jim Bouton's controversial new book," in Rochester to join the minor league team there.)

Jim this is Baney and I am still a fan. You think these guys are hollering now. Wait till I write my book. After your playing days you can be my advisor for a percentage.

Dick Baney

I thought you'd like to know about the comment of Sal Maglie. He's now a club official (general manager, in fact) with the Class A Niagara Falls Pirates in the New York-Penn League. . . . I sent a columnist on our sports staff to ask him what he thought about your book, and he said: (read carefully)

"I never listen to anything Bouton writes, and I never read anything he says."

> Sincerely,
> John Hanchette
> Niagara Falls *Gazette*
> *Niagara Falls, N.Y.*

Keep wondering why Mr. Kuhn keeps calling in the wrong people—why not Dooley Womack? That name has just got to be bad for baseball.

> A Friend
> Pete O'Hara*
> *Philadelphia, Pa.*

At about the same time you were scaling Dixie Cup tops at the Polo Grounds, my son Jonathan (now 22) made an exquisite crayon drawing of John Antonelli and sent it to him, hoping at the least for an autograph. He never got an answer.

In those days Jonathan (my son) was a devout candidate for The Establishment, devoted to baseball, art, family and school. Today he lives with his long hair, two cats and a girl in Los Angeles dedicating all his energies to the overthrow of everything by any means necessary.

I blame Antonelli.

> Sincerely,
> Robert Alan Aurthur
> *East Hampton, N.Y.*

I just bought your book "Ball Four." I really do enjoy it. It has entertainment—humor—dirty words E.T.C. The pictures were good also.

Fondly,
Dave Migdal
Syosset, N.Y.

I would like to comment on your seeming effort to destroy the halo that surrounds a Mantle or a Babe Ruth, etc., in context with what is happening to our country as a whole—yours is just another step in the grand strategy to discredit everything we learned to respect and sometimes worship when we were youngsters. . . . Whether you were right or wrong about Mantle, Houk, and the rest is irrelevant. What is relevant is that you impeached your own character more than the character of those you describe in your book.

Sincerely,
Sgt. A. E. Abramson*
Patrick AFB, Fla.

I, on the other hand, enjoyed it.

Best,
Michael Burke
[President,
New York Yankees]

9

WRITING BOOKS
FOR FUN AND PROFIT

Long ago, when I was a baseball player, I would tell my salary to any newspaperman who asked. This infuriated baseball management. The reason this infuriated baseball management is that it likes to keep salaries secret. Not big salaries. When the Yankees paid Mickey Mantle $100,000, they wanted everybody to know it. The Baltimore Orioles make no secret about what they pay Frank Robinson. But when some front office is trying to slip a second-year shortstop a fast $10,500 contract, it doesn't want anybody to notice.

Besides, if salaries were public, players could compare and one could say, "Now look here. You're paying that SOB five grand more than I'm getting and he hit twenty points less." The next thing you know, salaries would begin to be fair. As it is now, it isn't necessarily the best player who gets the most money. It's the best bargainer.

A classic example on the Yankees was Moose Skowron, a good first baseman (well, a good *hit-*

ting first baseman) and a lousy negotiator. Before Tony Kubek, the shortstop, turned establishment, he pointed out that although Moose was much the better player, Andy Carey, the hard-headed third baseman, always made more money. He made it because he was a better negotiator.

I used to give out my salary for a lot of reasons. One was that when I held out, as I did a couple of times with the Yankees, I wanted everybody to know I wasn't being unreasonable. If you *didn't* tell what you made and what you were asking for, management would leak it to the press that you were asking to duplicate the federal budget. Another is that Phil Linz, Tom Tresh, Joe Pepitone and I agreed as minor leaguers to always tell the truth about our salaries. (After a while only Linz and I were still telling.) Finally, there is the fact that I try to be honest. I really do. It didn't hurt me to tell what my salary was and maybe it helped some rookie someplace to know what he was shooting for.

Now the dilemma. I've written a best seller. A lot of people would like to know how much money you make when you do that. It's a lot, and unfortunately money makes people sly. I'm not sure why. Maybe because they figure on a little income-tax cheating. What the hell, it's tempting. Maybe I ought to get sly too. I mean I'm no longer in baseball and I don't have to protect myself from general managers anymore. On the other hand, it would be inconsistent to suddenly go secret. I don't believe that consistency is necessarily a man's greatest asset. In this case, though, I can't think of a single reason, outside of slyness, to hold back now. (I revealed my TV salary for the same reason. ABC wasn't happy either.) Maybe the whole world would be better if everybody knew how much money everybody else was making.

The trouble is that getting paid for writing a best seller is different than signing a baseball contract. It's a lot more complicated. In fact, it turns out there are two separate amounts involved. The first is what you think you're going to get. The second is what you actually get. The first figure is arrived at by making a fair and reasonable estimate of sales, the honesty and efficiency of the publisher and your own agent, then adding the terms of the contract and the righteousness of man. The second reflects the reality of the situation. It's a reality that is first difficult to comprehend and finally difficult to face.

I have always thought that baseball was a strange and inefficiently run business, shot through with stupidity, bullheadedness, nepotism and, yes, even dishonesty. The reason baseball calls itself a game, I believe, is that it's too screwed up to be a business. Well, it's hard to believe—at least it was for me—but publishing is even more of a game than baseball, at any rate the part of publishing I came in contact with. There were times during the year or so in which I dealt closely with the people who worked for World, publishers of *Ball Four,* when I seriously wondered how some of them managed to find their way to work in the morning and home again at night. (Only one baseball player I know ever had this problem. After he got lost a few times his wife would drive him to and from the ball park.)

The difficulties with World started early on, probably the day we signed the contract. It's difficult to explain what makes you sign with one publisher instead of another. Usually it's only a matter of money. Somebody offers you $75,000. Somebody else offers $100,000. You take the $100,-000. That's not what happened here. I mean Sandy Koufax I wasn't. At the time I signed the book contract, I had just spent almost two years in the minor leagues. No one was buying a big name when they bought Jim Bouton.

I was going to start the 1969 season with the Seattle Pilots, an expansion team. There was no guarantee I would make the club. So no one who would contemplate buying the book could possibly know exactly what he was going to get. Obviously, some of my history with the Yankees would be of interest. Nevertheless any publisher would be paying for what amounted to a pig in a poke. I did not demand, nor expect to get, very much money. The way it worked out, two publishers offered $10,000 as an advance against royalties. (Another later said he would have offered the same had he been given the opportunity. The reason he wasn't was that he first wanted something on paper. I didn't know exactly what to give him, so he got nothing.)

That was the money involved, all of it. It's why I was amused later on to be accused of trying to make a publishing killing at the expense of baseball. At the time the book was started I had no way of knowing that I would make a nickel more than that $10,000. Indeed, only a fraction of that would be mine. Ten percent came off the top for the agent's fee. And, since my agreement with Leonard Shecter was that we would split the proceeds down the middle, it can be accurately said that I wrote the book for $4,500.

Every man, I suppose, has a price. I don't know what mine is or if I have one. I do know, though, that $4,500 isn't it.

A word of explanation here about advances against royalties. Books are sold on a royalty arrangement, so much to the author for each book sold. There is usually a sliding scale, going, most times, up to 15 percent of the retail price. If you don't sell enough books to cover the advance, you don't have to pay it back. That's the advantage of a big advance. If the book is a bomb, you get to keep the advance anyway. Of course, if the book is a runaway success, the advance is academic. It was not academic for me, certainly not at the beginning. In fact, I didn't think $4,500 was bad pay at all.

There were two main reasons for choosing World to publish *Ball Four* (which was tentatively titled

Baseball Journal). One was that the top editor there, Ed Kuhn, and his associate, Bob Gutwillig, were the ones who were given credit for bringing in the highly successful Jerry Kramer-Dick Schaap book, *Instant Replay*. Experience counts. The other reason is that Kuhn had written to Shecter, whose work he knew, asking if he wanted to take a hard look at sports in America and write a book about it. Shecter had, in fact, recently finished just such a book. He took Kuhn's title suggestion and called it *The Jocks*. Bobbs-Merrill published. Shecter also told Kuhn that he had a different book in mind, something he wanted to do with an unknown baseball player, one Jim Bouton. Kuhn bought it. There wasn't a word on paper, just a promise to deliver a book. I gave Kuhn points for that. I might even say I respected him.

The book biz being what it is these days, in a matter of months Kuhn was gone from World. So was Gutwillig. And so it goes. It may be just a rumor that World Publishing had been in terrible trouble and that *Ball Four* bailed it out. No matter. By this time the editor was Peter Ritner.

Ritner made me feel right at home. He reminded me of every general manager I ever knew. When a general manager puts his arm around you and tells you he's your friend, has your interests at heart and reminds you he might just as well be your father, check your wallet.

Ritner, a large, one could say bountiful, man, who had trouble buying shirts he could keep buttoned at the neck, was as warm and sincere as any general manager I had ever met. Despite this warmth and sincerity, we decided we'd be better off taking the book elsewhere. It is not an unusual procedure for an author to buy back his book by returning the advance in midstream, especially when he is suddenly confronted with a new set of editors. But Ritner wouldn't let loose. I've always wondered why. I suppose it was just stubbornness, because at that point he could only have seen some one hundred manuscript pages and I have reason to doubt he'd read them.

In lieu of returning the book to us, Ritner said he would give us an additional $10,000 advance. This would show his sincerity, his faith in us and his willingness to invest in a proper advertising budget.

Now here's what a poor, ignorant baseball player found out about advertising budgets in the publishing industry. The bigger the investment a company has in a book, the more it's willing to spend in order to recoup this investment. So the books that are most heavily advertised are not necessarily the best books. They're the ones that have been most expensive in terms of advance. (It's like the big bonus rookie getting many more chances than the talented sandlotter.) Of course, if the book suddenly catches on and hits the bestseller list, the advertising budget soars. A book doesn't get on the best-seller list because it's advertised—at least not usually. It's advertised because it's on the best-seller list. Except that *Ball Four* wasn't advertised much even after it got on the best-seller list. That's another story I'll get to a bit later.

We agreed to accept the additional $10,000. As an article of faith, of course. Then the other shoe was dropped. This was still the winter of 1969–70. The other shoe said that *Ball Four* would be published in November. Beautiful. A diary of the 1969 baseball season wasn't going to come out until *after* the 1970 baseball season and well into the football season. To say we were outraged is to say The Flood was caused by a shower.

We told Peter Ritner he no longer owned *Ball Four* and the next place we would see him was in court. I mean how the hell do you deal with that kind of logic? You might as well print the books and bury them in some graveyard at midnight. What a publishing coup! Well, yes, Peter Ritner admitted. However, it would be very expensive to get out a book in only four or five months. The costs would be incalculable, prohibitive, impossible. However, if we would agree to accept $5,000 less in advance, perhaps we could bring the book out in May. Naturally this would entail triple overtime, prohibitive expenses, etc. But because he, Peter Ritner, liked us, Bouton and Shecter, he would do it. And hang the costs, overtime, and prohibitive etc. All it would cost us was the $5,000. We sighed, then agreed.

Then came the matter of editing. In an interview with Cleveland Amory in the *Saturday Review*, Peter Ritner let it be known that he was the editor of *Ball Four*. In fact, there was no editor at all. This is the way many books are published these days, I am told. Shecter and I edited *Ball Four*—twice. The first time was before it went to the publisher. The second time was after their copyreader got through with it.

I don't know the name of the copyreader, and I wouldn't tell if I did. In any case, World had struck again. It had assigned a person to copyread and cut the manuscript who got his (or her) knowledge and attitudes toward sports out of Jack Armstrong. The result was that every single passage which told some truth, every passage that may possibly have been considered tough, or funny or sexy, was neatly excised. Example: The section in which I talked about the Yankees staying out late and partying whenever they played in Los Angeles was crossed out and this note was attached to the margin: "Is this possible?" Nah, I made it up.

An incredible job was done on the manuscript. If we had allowed these changes to stand, *Ball Four* would never have been heard of. We could have changed the title to *Peter Rabbit Goes to the Ballgame*. We wore out two erasers just restoring what the World copyreader had taken out. (I would, by the way, like to say a kind word here about Mike Marshall, pitcher. Marshall gave us some brilliant help. In what could only have been a labor of love, he went through the first complete draft of the book, indexing every anecdote, every conversation, every appearance of every player, on yellow legal paper. He pointed out every duplication, every point made more than once, every bit of literary overkill. He saved us an unimaginable amount of time and work.)

After all the arguing, the book didn't come out in May. It didn't come out the first week in June. It didn't come out June 12, which Peter Ritner swore up and down was publication date. It didn't come out until June 19. The timing called for the book to come out on the heels of the printing of excerpts in *Look*. It was weeks late and well after the shit had hit the fan. There was a great demand for books, but even by June 19 you could buy it only in New York. For a long time there were no books in Seattle, there were no books in Houston, there were no books in Philadelphia for goodness' sakes. Maybe worst of all, books that were supposed to be sent to me, so that I could give them out to my quivering teammates, were "lost." I personally had to carry two boxes of books with me from New York to Atlanta. You know what a box of books weighs? No wonder I was pitching lousy.

It was during this period that I'd call up World and holler at almost anybody who would answer the phone. Sometimes, I admit, this was only some poor little secretary. Just for that, Ritner wrote a letter to Theron Raines, our agent, the last line of which read, "It makes you wonder if his [my] real ambition isn't to be a Spanish inquisitor rather than a baseball pitcher." Boy, I *knew* the guy never read any books. All I ever wanted were some copies of *Ball Four*. I never asked for any goddam confessions.

The troubles went on right to the end. World told us that 195,000 books had been printed—no more. Then they told *Publishers' Weekly* that 260,000 had been printed and shipped. How could that happen? Well, apparently some of the people at World lie a lot.

At this writing there is no way we can tell how many books were actually sold. Of course, a publisher would never cheat a writer. Wouldn't be ethical, you know. What we can suspect, though, is that however many were sold, there could have been more. That's because there were no ads taken by World after the month of September. "I admit," Peter Ritner was to say, "that I am not satisfied with our ad campaign." What ad campaign? There never was one. It was only after some serious arm twisting that we were able to get a miserable little program for September. After that —nothing. It was as though World didn't *want* to sell any more books. Why that should be, I can't imagine. Maybe it's just the book biz.

Now to return to my original premise: the amount of money I *thought* I was going to get. Assuming we got the truth and *Publishers' Weekly* got the lie, we'll say that only 195,000 were printed and all were bought and paid for. (When

I think of how many more could have been sold around Christmas had there been more books and more ads, I grit my teeth in frustration.) On that basis, we can work up a little chart.

Royalties:	5,000 at $ .695 [1]	$ 3,475.00
	5,000 at $ .86875 [2]	4,343.75
	185,000 at $1.0425 [3]	192,862.50
Paperback sale to Dell Publishing [4]		100,000.00
Sale to *Look* [5]		13,000.00
Book-of-the-Month sale (alternate) [6]		5,000.00
Syndication (newspapers) [7]		1,000.00
I'm Glad You Didn't Take It Personally [8]		40,000.00

Total $359,681.25

[1] and [2] These figures represent 10 percent and 12½ percent of the first 10,000 books sold. That's 10 and 12½ percent of the $6.95 price. Hilariously, in its first statement to us, World efficiently credited these percentages on the basis of a $7.95 sale price, thus overpaying us by $1,125. They read it here first.

[3] After sales of 10,000, the royalty percentage goes to 15 percent.

[4] This sale was actually $200,000. The usual agreement is that the publisher receives one half of the paperback money. It is possible, although not likely, that enough paperbacks will be sold to cover this in royalties and then we would get more.

[5] This is a total payment. All rights to pre-publication sales are usually retained by the author.

[6] The original payment was $10,000. The publisher gets half. If enough books are sold through Book-of-the-Month we will get additional payment.

[7] Original payment was $1,000 here. Publisher gets half. But I'm sure, since so many papers ran excerpts of *Ball Four*, there will be at least this much involved.

[8] If there were no *Ball Four*, there would have been no *I'm Glad You Didn't Take It Personally*. We got a $40,000 advance (such is fame) for this book. So I feel it is proper to add this to the total.

That's not all mine, of course. First, 10 percent, $35,968.13, goes to the agent. That leaves $323,713.12, half for me, half for Shecter; $161,856.56 each. So much for expectations. The reality was somewhat different.

What was involved was some interesting legerdemain by World. The final figures are not yet available but I'll bet they show we sold considerably fewer than 195,000 books. I started to get this uneasy feeling when Peter Ritner began mumbling about getting returns that were, by some miracle, just about matching new sales. So there we were, Ritner said, sitting with 10,000 books in the warehouse, and what was the use of advertising a book that was now being returned by dealers? Well, maybe if there was advertising there would be fewer returns. . . . All academic. There was no advertising.

Then there was this dandy little item. It turned out there was a clause in the original contract which read as follows: "On copies sold for export, and on copies sold at a special discount of 50 percent or more from the U.S. retail list price, such as sales in bulk to recognized book clubs or reading circles, or to organizations outside regular book-selling channels, a royalty of 10 percent of the amount which the publisher receives [will be paid to the author]."

Now Theron Raines is not exactly a virgin in the book business. Among his clients are such best-selling authors as James Dickey (*Deliverance*) and Rod Thorpe (*The Detective*). He's arranged a few contracts. And he took this clause to mean that the royalty could only be cut to 10 percent of sale price if the books were sold outside of regular channels. This is a considerable cut, by the way. Ten percent of a book sold at 50 percent discount (the sale price of the book was $6.95) amounts to $.348 as opposed to the $1.0425 we would get ordinarily. That's a difference of almost $.70 per book. It can add up. Still, if you think the special discount is going to only special places, well, what the heck.

The heck came later. In our first statement from World there was a little item of 39,484 books sold "wholesale," the majority of them, we were to discover, to ordinary book outlets, so that our royalty, which should have been $41,162.07, came to only $13,718.

Let's examine what's involved here. Under ordinary circumstances book publishers sell books to retail outlets at anywhere from 40 to 48 percent discount. Let's call it 44 percent on average. This means that World gets $3.89 per book and pays us a regular royalty so that their proceeds come to $2.85 per book. Now, when they sell a book at 50 percent discount (or $3.475) and pay us a royalty of only $.348, their proceeds are $3.13 per book, a net gain of $.28 per book. That too can add up. On 50,000 books it's $14,000.

Of course only a cad would believe that World would take advantage of such a situation. Call me cad. We thought about the whole thing for a while, fought with World about it for a while longer, and sued. The first thing we did was get an injunction against the early distribution of the paperback. How we were able to do this is a long and rather dull story. But it was our only weapon and we were able, after an unimaginable amount of shouting at each other through expensive attorneys, to force a settlement. Most of it involved going to arbitration about those wholesale books. Given the attitude of most arbitration (split the difference), there is going to be a rather large slice taken in our beautiful dream.

Another huge slice will, naturally, be taken by the federal government. And the state. And the city. But it's always been my ambition to have a tax bill large enough to complain about. I've been told by businessmen that when you've got a big tax bill, some pretty good things must be happening to you. And I'm slowly turning from a pitcher into a businessman. Had to.

That wasn't all of it. World has a knack for piling on indignities. And I'll never think of Louisville, Kentucky, without remembering that. The way it happened, I was on tour peddling the book, signing copies in bookstores, appearing on television—things like that. Mostly I was going to large cities. But then I was told I had to go to Louisville, just had to. It meant, with bad connections and all, I would have to spend a Saturday away from home. But there was this big store, see, and all these other stores and all this big demand for me. So I went to Louisville, spent a lonely four hours in W. K. Stewart, a rather small bookstore at that, and signed a grand total of twenty books. I was grumbling to a lady who helped run the store about wasting a day and about how wrong World was to send me there, and she said, oh no, World wasn't wrong. *I had to come to Louisville*. The reason was that Frank Beard, the golfer, had not. Frank Beard, author, with Dick Schaap, of *Pro*, had agreed, apparently, to an autograph session at W. K. Stewart. Elaborate preparations had been made and it was a lovely party in every respect but one. Beard didn't show up. So W. K. Stewart sued World. In settlement of the suit, World agreed to produce a different jock. Someone named Jim Bouton.

10

THE MAKING OF A
SOCIAL LEPER

When I was a boy in Chicago I once tried to get Alvin Dark's autograph in Wrigley Field. I leaned over the fence near the dugout and stuck out a pencil and scorecard. "Alvin, please," I said. "I'm a Giant fan, a *Giant* fan." And Alvin Dark said, "Take a hike, son. Take a hike."

I recounted this incident in *Ball Four*. When Dark heard about it he said, "Lies, all lies. I didn't even know Bouton when he was a kid."

All right, Alvin. Pay attention.

I was born, the first of three sons, to George Hempstead Bouton and Trudy Vischer Bouton in Newark, N.J., on March 8, 1939. My father, a business executive now, was attending night school at Columbia and selling pressure cookers for a living at the time. His ancestry is French and English. The first Boutons came to this continent with the Huguenots (French Protestants) in 1620. Presumably the name was originally pronounced Boo-TON, but it has been anglicized to BOW (as in bow-wow)-tin. The Vischers, my mother's parents, are of German and Dutch ancestry and emigrated to this country before she was born. There are inventors on both sides of the family. My mother's father, Alfred Vischer, Jr., invented the Flex-Seal pressure cooker. He also held patents on parking meters and soft-drink dispensing machines. My father's father, Edgar M. Bouton, held important patents on elevators. I never invented anything.

I spent most of the first fifteen years of my life in suburban Rochelle Park and Ridgewood, New Jersey. I don't remember ever wanting for anything in particular, yet I was always some kind of money hustler. I had newspaper routes, collected pop bottles door-to-door for the deposits involved, collected old newspapers in a wagon and saved them up for a junk dealer and like that. My brother Bob, almost two years younger than I, was usually my partner. I did about 80 percent of the work and gave him half the money. I like to feel it was because he was my younger brother and I felt sorry for him and the fact that he always got higher grades in school was a coincidence. Besides, I never applied myself to schoolwork the way he did. I could never tell whether he was simply always in less trouble than I or whether he was the family favorite.

When I was thirteen and living in Ridgewood I set up a business for me and Bob. I printed up cards in the school printshop. They read: "Odd Jobs. Baby sitting, car washing, dog washing, lawns mowed, painting. You name it, we'll do it."

Dad had bought a power mower and we paid for half of it out of our first thirty jobs or so. We got $4 a job, $2 for the front, $2 for the back. There were always ladies who tried to make us do extra for the $4. I remember one in particular who'd have us trimming her shrubbery, taking out the garbage, doing odd jobs. We'd do six or seven hours of work and come away with $4. Finally one day I screwed up enough courage to tell her that from now on she'd have to pay a dollar an hour for our labor. She was upset, but she paid up. This was good training for me later, when I had to deal with general managers.

I can't explain why I thought it was so important to earn money. I'm not even sure what I did with it. I do remember buying a long-term supply of Sugar Daddies. They were a terrific candy buy. Three Musketeers and Milky Ways would go down in a few seconds. Sugar Daddies cost the same five cents and lasted forty-five minutes. I bought about fifty Sugar Daddies and put them in my drawer underneath my underwear. I felt rich, independent and powerful.

I was always rather small as a boy. For a while I worried that I might turn out to be a midget. I used to cut out pieces of cardboard the shape of my heel and put two or three of them in each shoe. This was because of the girls. I must have been a fair athlete, though, because I made the eighth-grade baseball team when I was in the fifth grade. At those ages there is a lot of difference in size, so this was a fairly big deal. Bob Gamere, who was a Yankee announcer for a season, recalled recently that he went to Purple Heart in Rochelle Park and that we often played baseball on the same field. He says I wasn't a very good player but had a big mouth.

He might be right about the mouth, but it's not true that I wasn't a good player. He probably didn't like me just because I was a pain in the ass. I played every game as though it were a World Series. If my team lost, I'd cry. I'd scream at kids who made errors. I'd run across the field and kick my own teammate in the shins. I was a fiend.

I suppose that was part of why I played well. Because I *wanted* to. I'm not your great athlete who picks up a tennis racquet for the first time and is an ace in an hour. I found golf a difficult game. Still, when I was a caddy, I went out every Monday and worked my tail off until I became a pretty fair player. When I wasn't working, I was playing games. I had tremendous energy. I was always being chewed out for coming late for supper. I wore a lot of holes in my trousers and I often came home with grass stains all over and ripped shoes. My mother made some big scenes about that.

When I was fifteen my father's job took him to Chicago and I finished high school at Bloom Township in Chicago Heights, Illinois. This was going from a quite small school to a very large one and suddenly I couldn't even make the football or basketball team and I barely made the baseball team. I had thought I was a hotshot athlete. Instead I was a mess. This didn't stop me from trying, though, and as a result everybody began to call me Warmup Bouton. That's all I ever did, warm up. They even taped the name on my locker. They'd put the left fielder in to pitch, they'd put in the catcher, they'd pull a guy out of the stands for crissakes, and I'd still be warming up. I was the guy who sits on the bench and says, "Now coach, now?" and the coach says, "Not yet."

That first season, my sophomore year, I got into one game at the end of the season. The idea of that one was to let all those kids who hadn't played all season get into a game. I pitched five innings, gave up no hits. Big deal, the season was over. Also, I had the world's worst case of acne. And braces on my teeth. I was an absolute squirrel, and I often wondered why I should be alive. And that summer, for the first time since I could remember, I didn't play any baseball. I worked at the A & P stamping 2 for 39 on the Contadina tomato paste.

Now that I've put enough distance between me and those terrible times, I think the experience was good. The feelings I had of not being one of the guys, not being able to make the team, not dating cheerleaders, being the kind of kid that the athletes pointed at and snickered about, made me forever aware of the outsider, the underdog. It's the kind of thing that you remember every time you join in with the big boys, putting down the little guy. It has made me shut up more than once.

In trying to remember the things that marked me as a boy, besides my feelings of power in a candy store, I can think of very little. I remember one time on Halloween night, when I was about sixteen, a bunch of us were out throwing tomatoes at Michael Root's house. I wondered why we had singled him out. I'd always considered him a decent fellow. But there I was, at 2 A.M., throwing tomatoes like everybody else. The answer was, well, he's Jewish. Oh.

What I learned from that was mostly about myself. I learned how easy it was to be a part of a gang and do something terrible and still feel good to be part of it. Some of that mob thing goes on with baseball teams, too, and I remember when the Yankees would gang up on a writer—"nobody talk to this guy"—I made it a point to talk to him and be seen having lunch with him.

Growing up in New Jersey and Chicago suburbs the way I did, I never really encountered any blacks or any black problems. I would describe my parents as relatively conservative—politically, economically. Yet they were very conscious about instilling what I can only call an antiprejudice. I remember once in a department store, when I was about twelve, I picked up one of those fake nose and eyeglass things and was laughing at my image. My father snatched it away from me and pointed out very carefully that people might think I was making fun of Jews. I didn't even know what a

Jew was at the time and my dad apologized, explained, and told me he never wanted me to make fun of people, *any* people. I suppose that made an impression because I still remember it.

Although my folks were never particularly religious they managed to instill, I believe, some important basics. Most importantly, there was a lot of love. I knew all the time, and with certainty, that they loved me. I knew that no matter what I did, or what kind of trouble I got into, or how unpopular I was, they would support me. They've been of great help to me through the years. I never went through that stage where I said to hell with my parents, what do they know? Even now when I'm making a big decision I consult them—partly out of respect, but mostly because they almost always give good advice. Not only that, they listen to *me*. I like to think that in recent years I have even been able to shape some of their ideas on religion and politics.

At the same time, I picked up some conservative ideas from them that I had to unlearn later on. For a long time in my life I believed that what was good for General Motors was good for everybody. I watched my father work his way up in business after going to college at night. I saw him move from a salesman's job to a branch manager's job to an executive's job, each time making more money, and it seemed to me that was the system, and it worked. It was a long time before I began to think about the people who had the menial jobs, the people who were dead-ended, the people who couldn't move up because the system held them down. Eventually, of course, I was introduced to general managers and it wasn't much of a discovery to find out that business took as much as it could, gave as little as possible and that you had to fight your way through the corporate jungle in order to just stay even.

There are some things, though, that will not change. My father had to work his way through life and I had to work my way through mine. My father didn't buy me a car when I went to college. I had to buy one for myself. I approve. I'll send my kids to college and buy my daughter a big wedding if she wants one, but there will be no jobs for anyone in my real estate business and I won't try to get any of them a job in television. You can't make it because of your old man. That's why I didn't name my kid Jim Jr. I don't want him to be an extension of me. I want him to be his own person.

That's the way I grew up and I sort of think it's the one true way. I like to think it worked with me. I had a lot of drive and all that energy as a kid and I was tough to control. Still, I never went out and committed any crimes and I was always honest. I found it difficult, if not impossible, to lie, especially to my dad. If he asked me point-blank about something, even something I stood to get punished for, I'd tell and take my punishment. I'd like to think my kids do the same.

("I don't know what happened to you back early in your life," Harry Walker once told me. "I don't know your mom and dad. But something happened to make you the way you are. You just don't fit in and you're apart from things. You're separated from everyone else. This is bad. You've got to learn to fit in. I'm not so concerned about you, because you'll be all right. But your kids ... I'm afraid they may learn this from you. You've got to be careful when you're raising kids. They've got to learn to fit in.")

I should point out that my parents didn't raise three identical boys. Bob was the good guy and I was the bad guy. No one was sure about Pete, who is six years younger than I. What I remember most about Pete was that Bob and I would use him. We'd send him around ringing doorbells to scrounge cookies and other goodies by saying he was an orphan. Once, when he was bugging us, we tied him to his bed for a whole afternoon. It's wonderful to have older brothers.

Probably I was blamed for that particular escapade and probably I should have been. That's the way I was. The things that marked me as a boy were the acne, the braces, being called Warmup, being the bad guy. I felt myself, during that period, as an outsider, and probably this helped turn me on to the underdog. I mean I couldn't root for the Yankees, not for a team that always won. I had to root for the Giants. As all New Yorkers of a certain age know, Giant fans were all flakes.

The next year I decided to forgive everybody and try baseball one more time. It was then I discovered how much help a sports writer could be. I went out for American Legion ball that summer and the first practice was called for two o'clock. Naturally I was there at two. I was the only one, except for the coach, a fellow named Earl DeTella. All the big stars knew they really didn't have to show up the first few days, or on time. They didn't have to earn any job. And when opening day came and everybody thought that Jerry Colangelo, who is now general manager of the Phoenix Suns, a basketball team, would be the starter, DeTella said no, Bouton gets this one. "He was here first. You guys didn't show. He works hard. We'll let him pitch." This made a tremendous impression on me. I won't say that's the reason I always hustled after that, because I always hustled before. But it gave me a sense of reward; I began to understand that if you hustle all the time something good could happen sometimes.

When it came to pitch the championship game, I pitched for DeTella and lost it. Then there was a consolation game against a really easy team. It was a chance to rack up a lot of strikeouts and look good. Colangelo thought he was going to get this game too. He didn't. Warmup Bouton did, knuckleball and all. (Oh yes, I did throw the knuckleball in those days. It wasn't until I went into the Yankee farm system that I found out I wasn't just a young junkball pitcher.)

Which is where the newspaperman came in. Because DeTella gave me the chance, I was able to make some impressions on people. One of them was a local reporter named John Meyers. At the end of the American Legion season he wrote a marvelous story in the form of a letter to the high-school coach. He said, in effect, that there was a new number one starting pitcher in town, coach. He said it wasn't Jerry Colangelo, it was Jim Bouton. The kid earned it this season in American Legion ball. He said the coach just had to pitch the kid. And that's the way it worked out. Sports writers were big men in that part of the country.

I don't think I hustled as part of any grand plan. I hustled because it never occurred to me not to. I remember once in college we had to run laps around the field. When I was through running mine the coach asked me if I'd done my laps. Sure, I said. "I didn't see you do them," he said. So I ran two more, right away, quick. I could have stood there and argued. As several general managers can tell you, I'm not exactly averse to arguing. But in that kind of situation, well, what's a little more hard work?

I went to Western Michigan with the assurance that if I looked good on the freshman team, I would get a scholarship my sophomore year. I did get it, but when I got the offer to sign with the Yankees for a three-year $30,000 contract, I took it. My mom was against it at first. She had read about all those bonus players who never amounted to anything. Still, I felt I was better off with the $30,-000 than without it. Dad understood how itchy I was to try it, and it's a funny thing, as soon as I signed, I seemed to get a lot more confidence in myself. Along about this time my acne went away and the braces came off my teeth and my name was in the local paper and I felt, well, like the ugly duckling that was starting to turn into a swan.

It's hard to describe how delighted I was to play professional baseball. When I first started college the adviser kept asking, "What do you want to be?" My answer was that I didn't know. I started with a business major, switched to liberal arts, then back to business, then back to liberal arts again. The only thing I was sure of was that I didn't want to be a salesman. I saw myself as more of an entrepreneur, but I didn't know of what. Baseball was the perfect way to postpone the decision. (My dad had made me promise to go to college while I played ball and I did go for four winters, although I'm still short of a degree.)

I got along very well with the other young players in the minor leagues. Most minor leaguers are so insecure they tend to huddle together. Every once in a while, though, there'd be somebody from the old school. Like a pitcher named Dick Stewart in Greensboro. He used to get on me about all kinds of things, about how I warmed up, how I wore my uniform, my spikes, everything. I began to think, my God, maybe he's right. Maybe I only *think* I'm a real live baseball player. Then halfway through the season I had ten wins and he got his release. Looking back, I realize he was nothing but a frustrated old guy who realized his time was gone and he was jealous of me and wanted to make life difficult for me. The Frank Merriwell school of baseball would have it that the grizzled veteran always helps the young milk-cheeked rookie. Yeah, surrre.

Another thing I found out early on was that when you were told the only way to make it to the big leagues was to keep your nose clean, keep good hours and stay away from girls, you were being bullshitted. All those things wouldn't do you a bit of good unless you could hit. And if you could, you didn't have to pay any attention to the rules.

Here's something that might be counted as significant. I remember playing on a Chicago amateur team against a prison team. My brother Bob was our equipment man. One of the guards asked him what was in the bat bag and he said, "Guns." They emptied every one of our bags before they were satisfied he was kidding.

Then, when I was in the minors, we were coming across the border from Canada in our bus. It was a Customs man or an Immigration man that woke me up and asked where I was born. It struck me as a ridiculous question. So I said Jablib, Wisconsin. I'm not sure there *is* a Jablib, Wisconsin.

He didn't seem to notice. Then he asked me what we were carrying on the bus. I said, "Guns and marijuana." That did it. "Everybody off the bus!" he said. It took our manager thirty minutes to talk him out of going through everything with a comb. About 90 percent of the guys were steamed at me, the rest thought it was a hell of a gag.

If I were a Customs man I'd search anybody who said he was carrying baseball bats and balls, and let anybody go who said guns and marijuana.

I enjoyed all the crazy things that young guys do in the minors. Like one night in Victoria, Texas, Paul Erickson, a righthanded pitcher, Hal Stowe, a lefthanded pitcher, and, I think, Jim Burton, a righthanded pitcher, and I got into a game of, would you believe, strip poker. This was a special kind of strip poker, though. The rules were that we would play until one of us had no clothes at all. Then the game would stop, everyone would put shoes on and we would do one lap around Eddie Brown's motel. This involved about fifty or sixty yards along the heavily traveled main road, around the Coke machine and the ice machine, past the restaurant and back. It was about one in the morning and there were still people about. That's why it was so much fun. I'll never forget the sight of Hal Stowe's bare ass bobbing up and down in front of me. Before it was over, all four of us were running around the outside of the motel, stark naked.

It sounds insane, I know, and perhaps it really is. Maybe being a minor-league baseball player makes you insane. Maybe you just have to be crazy to be a minor-league baseball player. Whatever it was you needed, I had it. I walked around the streets with the guys, goofed off, picked up girls. And I wasn't exactly famous for reading books, not in the minors anyway. I was just one of the guys.

This was also true in my first years with the Yankees. I was, for goodness' sakes, a *fan* of people like Mickey Mantle and Roger Maris. If Mantle was rough with kids who wanted his autograph, or Maris was giving the finger to the fans, I'd say, "My goodness, those fans ought not to be bothering Roger and Mickey," and I'd laugh self-consciously. Friends would ask me if Maris was loafing and I'd say, "No, he's just conserving his energy." I was awed just sitting in the same room with those guys.

Things changed slowly. I wish I could lay out a graph of my mind, like the stock market averages, with little arrows pointing to peaks and lows, indicating events that caused them. I can't. I don't think anybody can. I just started to change. Despite what some people believe, the changing had nothing to do with how I was doing on the field. I was going pretty good when I started doing my Crazy Guggenheim bit, and I was mugging Frank Fontaine around the batting cage one day and a few of the guys, especially Maris, got mad at me.

Quit fooling around, you got a ball game today. That's not only a bad rap, it's a dumb one. Nobody ever took the game more seriously than I. You could check it out. Just count the times my hat fell off when I was pitching.

There were other things. After two or three years of playing with guys like Mantle and Maris, I was no longer awed. I started to look at those guys as people and I didn't like what I saw. They were fine as baseball heroes. As men they were not quite so successful. At the same time I guess I started to rub a lot of people the wrong way. Instead of being a funny rookie, I was a veteran wise-guy. I reached the point where I would argue to support my opinion and that didn't go down too well either.

This is not to say I had no friends on the Yankee ball club. As I explained in *Ball Four*, the nature of the game makes having close friends emotionally dangerous; you never know when they're going to be traded to Anchorage or farmed to Timbuktu. And that's only if you aren't both trying for the same position. Still, I never had a roommate I didn't get along with and I think Fritz Peterson and I, for one example, will always be good friends. I also got along well with Steve Hamilton, although he was much more conservative politically than I, and his opinions about guns are well ... ugh. Steve went on the Dick Cavett show and put the knock on *Ball Four*. I forgive him. You can knock my book and still be my friend. (After

215

the book came out Whitey Ford said I was the most disliked guy on the club, and the only thing I can say to that is, come, come, my good man, not as long as there was a Jim Coates. I'm always saying things like that. It's why I was one of the most disliked guys on the club.)

Another guy I felt close to on the Yankees was Tony Kubek. He got some fame and a lot of static for being an iconoclast. (Being an iconoclast in baseball means he revealed his salary in *Sports Illustrated*.) When the Yankees put him on the carpet for talking too much, Kubek backed off. He became an establishment type and today he's Game of the Week and things like that. At any rate, Kubek was one of the first people to interview me on the tube about the book. He was really rather tough, and a case could be made that he didn't give me enough of an opportunity to rebut. Still, I don't think interviewers should be bland, and I think he was right to get on me if he disagreed with me.

There was an interesting sidelight to this little contretemps. Kubek had interviewed me on the pre-game Game of the Week show. The next time I saw him I asked if he had taken any abuse for putting me on the air.

"Well, the Commissioner was upset," Kubek said. "He said it wasn't a very good idea to have you on."

I asked what Kubek said to that.

"I said, well, I took a stand *against* the book. I didn't say that you had done a good thing."

Then Kubek let the cat out of the bag.

"You know, I can't understand why he was upset," he said. "After all, his office cleared you as a guest in the first place."

"How's that?" I said naïvely.

"Well, we called the Commissioner's office to find out if it would be all right to have you on and somebody there, I don't know who, but one of his people, said fine, go ahead."

"Gee Tony," I said, "I didn't know the Commissioner had to approve your shows."

With that, Kubek had the good grace to retire in confusion.

It wasn't just the gradual perception of the kind of crap that goes on in baseball that changed me the most. I think the greatest influence on me came from just being in New York. I was like a dry sponge, me and my empty head. And the people in New York helped fill it up. I started listening to guys talk about the war in Vietnam, civil rights, politics, guys who seemed to know what they were talking about, guys who grew up in New York and were hip and sharp and had principles that had been shaped at a very early age. I mean like some of the reporters around the club ("Watch out for the goddam newspapermen," the Yankees used to say), guys like George Vecsey, Steve Jacobson, Stan Isaacs, Vic Ziegel and some foul fiend named Shecter ("especially that fucking Shecter").

11

RETURN OF THE NATIVE

The end product of that long road is James Alan Bouton, tint in his hair, makeup on his face, a smile on his lips, a Channel 7 emblem over his heart and a microphone in his hand. This is success? As baseball managers like to say, it's too early to tell. In the meantime, what has gone before has pushed me in a certain direction. I have taken the path of the chipmunks.

Chipmunkism is a school of sports journalism my friends in the business belong to. It requires a tough, irreverent, amusing attitude toward sports. It led me to do this kind of TV piece after Satchel Paige, the black pitcher, was elected to a side corridor of the Hall of Fame.

Commissioner Bowie Kuhn was asked if this meant Satch was officially in the Hall of Fame. The Commissioner said, "Technically no."

He said it's only one of many separate exhibits. If you count being part of a side exhibit—*I'm* in the Hall of Fame. . . . Baseball says there's this rule that you have to have a minimum of ten years in the majors to qualify. And everyone knows you can't change a rule.

Baseball's just not doing the right thing. I mean, even Willie Mays isn't sure it's the right thing.

When told he wasn't really in the Hall of Fame, Satchel Paige said, "To tell you the truth, I don't know what this is all about."

What it's all about, Satch, is that you're going into the back of the Hall of Fame, near the kitchen.

Any card-carrying chipmunk would have pounced on the deal the Pittsburgh Pirates made when they were allowed to sneak Mudcat Grant past the New York Mets during the 1970 season. It was, I thought, the kind of deal which double-crosses the fans, hurts the players involved and casts a very bad light on the game. This was my bit on it:

Why did the Mets lose the pennant? Some people think they lost it early in the season when Cleon Jones didn't hit. Others think they lost it late in the season when Tom Seaver didn't win his twenty-five games. I don't agree with either of those theories. I think the Met management lost it.

They lost it because they let relief pitcher Mudcat Grant go to the Pittsburgh Pirates when they could have had him first for the $20,000 waiver price. Grant was having a great year with twenty-four saves and a 1.7 Earned Run Average when the Mets let him pass.

Several days later the Mets selected instead relief pitcher Dean Chance, who was having a poor year. His Earned Run Average was 4.7. . . . If the Mets had taken a Grant instead of a Chance there might still be a pennant race.

And how could all those other teams along with the Mets turn down Grant for only $20,-000? Was there a secret agreement made to let him pass by all those teams? Shouldn't the Commissioner be asking the same question?

There's no reason you can't try to be amusing even when the news appears a bit grim. Take this:

The honeymoon appears to be over for my Houston Astro teammate, outfielder Jim Wynn, and his lovely wife Ruth. Seems the Wynns were celebrating their seventh wedding anniversary when Ruth stabbed her hubby in the stomach with a four-inch steak knife. He is in the hospital and his condition is satisfactory. Jimmy, trying to keep the embers glowing, has refused to press charges. And

Ruth should know that the traditional gift on your seventh anniversary is not steel, but copper.

And sometimes you can make a point with a funny story:

> In Nairobi, Kenya, one of the leading soccer teams spent $3,000 on witch doctors last year. Sports leaders there have tried to discourage witchcraft as well as the practice of players painting their bodies with pig fat to ward off evil spirits.
>
> Athletic teams in our country, of course, are much too sophisticated to travel with witch doctors and wear pig fat. Our teams travel with clergymen and wear medals.
>
> In Africa when the team loses they get rid of the witch doctor. Over here when they lose the clergyman stays and they get rid of the player. I like their way better.

Now I don't know if this sort of thing is doing Channel 7 much good. I do know that the month I started working NBC and CBS news fell below ABC in the ratings for the first time in the recorded history of mankind. Also, Frank Gifford over at CBS changed his hairstyle from the conventional straight-back to the sort of down-and-mussed-up-in-front-mod style that I happen to wear. I must admit that I think Gifford's new hairstyle is probably just a coincidence.

Not that I would want anyone to think that there was an instant love affair between me and all my millions of viewers. Far from it. Apparently I drove some of them right up the wall.

Like the time greenies got into the news I said that I'd taken them, and thought they improved my performance about 5 percent. Unfortunately, I said, in my particular case that wasn't nearly enough.

There followed a bunch of telephone calls. One of the callers said I had the IQ of a child. He didn't say how old.

Another time I did what I thought was a funny piece about the women tennis players who were starting their own tour. They denied they had been inspired by women's lib, and I suggested that if things didn't go well they might have to go that way eventually. I also said it might be a good thing. Imagine a bra-less tennis tournament.

The next day this man actually stopped me in the street—Forty-eighth Street and Madison Avenue. "You're Jim Bouton, aren't you?" he said.

I always answer yes to that question.

"Well, I want to tell you that I was offended and upset by your show last night."

I didn't know what he was talking about. "You were?" I said.

"Yes, I was. You know, I'm from Ridgewood, New Jersey, the same town you used to be from, and I want to tell you that my children and I were shocked by what you said they wore at those tennis tournaments."

"What are you *talking* about?" I said, glancing around for possible emergency help.

"You know what I'm talking about," he said. "You know exactly what I'm talking about."

"I'm sorry," I said, edging away. "I didn't talk about what people were wearing at tennis tournaments."

"Yes, you did," he said, "and I was offended by it."

Suddenly a light dawned. "Do you mean when I speculated on the possibility of a bra-less tournament?"

"That's right," he said. "It was disgusting. It was absolutely uncalled for and I'm never going to watch Eyewitness News again. It's just not the kind of thing that should go into a home."

"Gee, don't you think a bra-less tennis tournament would be fun?" I said.

"No I don't," he said, and strode off.

Everybody's a critic.

Especially the Yankees. It can safely be said that the Yankees don't like me. Strange, that. I was harder on the Yankee front office in *Ball Four* than I was on anybody. The front office—which has changed a lot of its personnel, I admit—forgave me. The ball club did not. Actually I didn't say anything at all negative about the players. But I did, as they like to say, "rip" the manager, and

Mantle and Howard, who were coaches. (A "rip" in baseball is anything that isn't pancakes with syrup.) Is it possible that players can be influenced by managers and coaches? Is it?

In any case, once I went to work for ABC I was very eager to see how the club would react to me as a broadcaster. So we called and said we were coming up to Yankee Stadium to do a series of interviews. We didn't say "we" was Jim Bouton. I didn't want anybody digging in on me.

When I got out of the car at the player entrance to the Stadium, the doorman said, "Oh God, Bouton's here. I got to see this." He and a lot of other people took off for the dugout. Pretty soon there was a large selection of ushers, peanut vendors, hot-dog salesmen, secretaries and ground-crew members huddled around the dugout. They were disappointed. It was a lousy show.

For one thing, Ralph Houk, the manager, had given word that I was not to be allowed in the clubhouse. I didn't take the hint. Maybe they don't like cameras in the clubhouse. So we set up just outside the dugout.

A lot of players ran by me on the way out to the field. They ran fast. Only one stopped. My left-handed friend, Fritz Peterson. "Jim, you know I love you," Fritz said. "But I just can't talk to you now. I just can't. It's unbelievable what's going on inside the clubhouse. There's all kinds of pressure."

I told Fritz I understood.

A lot of the pressure, I discovered later, came from Elston Howard. So okay. A lot of it also came from Pete Ward. I don't even *know* Pete Ward. All I could think was that he was trying to curry favor with the manager. (And it didn't do him any good. He was released this spring.) Pete Ward, for goodness' sakes.

Actually a couple of other people stopped by to visit with this ABC correspondent. One of them was Mike McCormick, the old Giant lefthander. We did a little interview. I'm afraid it wasn't a good one. We never put it on the air.

The other guy was Mike Kekich. He's young, also a lefthander and Fritz Peterson's roommate.

"Hey Jim," he said, "I'll talk to you."

"Nah, I don't want to get you into any more trouble than you're already in," I said.

"I don't care," he said. "I'll talk."

There must be something about lefthanded pitchers.

All during the time I was standing in front of the dugout Elston Howard was sitting maybe ten feet away, pretending I wasn't there. It really was a cheat on all those nice people who had rushed over to see my blood flow. I tried to catch his eye a few times, but he always managed to look away. Then, as I was walking through the stands on my way out, Howard stepped to the top of the dugout, raised his fist to the players on the field and shouted his appreciation of the way they had ignored me.

If Howard actually wanted to punch me out, he had another, even better, opportunity. This was during the football season and by the merest chance we suddenly ran into each other, nose to nose, eyeball to eyeball, all alone in a narrow corridor near the Giant dressing room in Yankee Stadium. I didn't know what to say. So I said, "Hi Ellie."

And Elston Howard said, "Hi."

You'd think that would have been it between me and the Yankees. You'd think I'd have quit exposing myself to their juvenile, insulting behavior. You'd think I'd say the hell with the Yankees, let's go Mets. Well, you'd be wrong. They don't call me Bulldog for nothing.

In the winter the club has what is called a Yankee Caravan. Its purpose is to sell tickets. ABC was invited to send a camera to a suite in the Americana Hotel. I had to go. Not too many press people felt that way. There were more players than, as they say, media men. ABC had the only camera in sight. Hardly anybody wants to buy tickets to Yankee games these days.

Gene Michael, the shortstop, came over to pay his respects. He was holding his hands as though he were hefting a couple of grapefruit. "You got a pair on you like this," he said. Why thank you Gene.

I was really there to get my confrontation with Ralph Houk over with before spring training. I thought that as one professional to another, he'd understand why it would be better for everybody if we cooled things off. The Yankees could use any publicity I gave them. And I could use any good interviews I could get.

Houk said I was right. He said he didn't hold any grudges. He said he wouldn't go on camera with me at this very moment, but that in time he might. In the meantime, he would try to ease things so that the players would talk to me in spring training. He said he really would try. Mike Burke, the Yankee president, happily performed before my camera and said that he too would try in the spring.

Trying wasn't enough. In the spring I did a gag interview with Fritz Peterson through a cyclone fence. That was it. ABC viewers in New York were therefore treated to four interviews with the Washington Senators, five with the Houston Astros, four with the New York Mets, and one with Fritz Peterson. I really must have sold a lot of tickets for the Yankees.

I had a great time with the Astros. They made me feel most welcome, and there was a marvelously nutty interview with Doug Rader, the third baseman, who suggested that Little Leaguers should actually live on a diet of bases, pitchers' mounds and bubble-gum cards.

Bubble-gum cards?

"Oh yes. They have lots of information on them about hitting and pitching."

That's another great thing about being a sportscaster. It keeps me in contact with all of that.

12.

THE GAME I LOVE

The spring of 1971 was the strangest time. For eleven years, the end of February meant packing up the kids and going off to Florida or Arizona. It meant running and sweating and doing pickups and that good hurt feeling your body gets when you're forcing it into shape. It meant that first tentative testing of the arm and feeling it get strong and that lovely sound the ball made when you were really able to begin popping it into the catcher's glove. It meant the renewal of old friendships and kidding around in the outfield and practical jokes and creative use of four-letter words. It meant sand in bed instead of just the usual cookie crumbs and it meant a renewal—this year, this would be the big one. It was hope and joy and high blue skies and the farther one gets away from it, the more beautiful it becomes.

But this was the season that comes to most of us, not just the last season, the one after that; the season that is no season and in February you are not packing, you are not sweating, you are not playing baseball. Lord, how I missed it! I knew I would. I also admit that when I heard that Bob Short, the owner of the Washington Senators, had expressed interest in me, the tops of my ears got red and itchy. Ah, I knew he wasn't serious. I mean he's got Curt Flood and Denny McLain and Mike Epstein and Ted Williams and Joe Foy and he was only kidding when he talked about adding another flake. However, it's not all that fanciful. I give you a quote from one T. Williams, manager. It's from the Washington *Star* of August 28, 1969, after Seattle had traded me to Houston:

> "I'll tell you what," Williams said on the bench last night in the Twins' Stadium, "next year Bouton might just be the best relief pitcher in the National League. I don't know why Seattle gave up on him, but I know his knuckler was almost unhittable against us. If I understood these waiver rules better, we would have had him."

Ahem.

Of course that was two years ago now, almost. And I think Short has a lot of nerve even thinking about getting me to return to baseball. I'm a big man in television. I'm an author. I'm nearly rich. Who needs baseball? Right? Well, I want to make one thing perfectly clear. If Short's talking, Jim Bouton is listening.

For the fact, the absolute, ever-loving blue-eyed fact, is that I'll always miss baseball. You can't give all your adult attention and striving to a single purpose and walk away from it without feeling a great deal of emptiness and even more sinking feeling. I'm not going to become a coach, though, and I'm not going to get drunk and cry tears about it.

Not long ago Roger Kahn, a writer who did not like *Ball Four*, wrote in *Esquire* about a player who was losing his skills and knew it. "It is something to cry about, being an athlete who does not die young," Kahn wrote. And all I could think was, bullshit. Only a man who never played the game could have written that line. It's fake, like the men who cry when they can no longer play baseball are fakes. You can miss baseball all right, but you can't miss it that much. You can't, you *don't* believe your life ends when you stop playing a game. Baseball isn't the only way of life. It's a game you play for fun and money and when the time comes you have to be able to walk away from it. This doesn't mean you can't carry in your head the things that were fun. I don't mean the usual things, the winning, the good pitch, the timely strikeout, the base hit. That's nice too. What sticks to *my* ribs, though, are the dumb things, the foolish camaraderie of the clubhouse, the easy, funny profanity, the practical jokes. I even enjoyed the cruelty and the grossness. As Larry Dierker once said after he had spent two weeks with his reserve army unit, "I come back all smiles. I can't wait for the same old nonsense."

He meant, for example, Doug Rader.

Rader played third base for the Houston Astros —wildly, even fiendishly. He was always making catches which required him to bounce on his head. The guys used to say he liked it because it happened to him all the time when he was a kid.

Rader lent something to the club, a happiness, a *joie*, that was fun when we were winning and desperately needed when we were losing. He had a knack for vilifying umpires in such an outrageous manner, they'd laugh instead of throwing him out of the game. "Hey ump, you got cataracts," he'd yell. Or, "I hope your balls rot off." On days of "big" games he'd walk around the clubhouse in his underwear, saying, "Greenie up, greenie up, men, got to greenie up for the big one." Before an unimportant game, he'd walk around saying, "To greenie or not to greenie, that is the question." And when *Ball Four* came out he warned me that if the Commissioner cracked down on greenies the withdrawal pains would be on my head.

Rader was often the butt of little jokes. Like once, when he was in a slump, Dierker and I pasted Band-Aids on his bat. He didn't notice until he was in the on-deck circle and the betting on the bench was he'd go berserk and try to kill both of us. Instead, he just laughed.

Guys around the club liked to tell Doug Rader army stories. One was about maneuvers his company was involved in. The captain was explaining that they were going to sneak around the "enemy" and attack from the rear. "Oh," said Rader, in happy recognition of the problem. "You mean dog style."

During another training exercise Rader's squad was assigned to capture a certain colonel. They failed, and trailed back to camp dirty and weary. There they encountered the colonel in the officer's mess. "Where the hell have you been?" Rader said. "We've been looking for you all day, you old sonovabitch."

Keith Lampard, the young outfielder who tells the story, says that Rader was probably the only man in the whole U.S. Army who could have gotten away with that.

Now I'd like to tell about Doug Rader making people throw up. If you throw up easily you'd better skip this part. The thing is that Rader *likes* to make people throw up—and I liked to watch him do it.

His favorite mark was J. Alou. (We called him J. or Jesus, never hay-soos, which is the way his name is supposed to be pronounced.) J. is one of the most delicate, sensitive, nicest men I have ever met. He'd walk a mile out of his way to drop a coin in some beggar's cup. He even liked Doug Rader—from a distance, that is. Up close, Rader made him nervous.

233

Now here's J. sitting at one end of the dugout and Rader, an evil gleam in his eye, approaches. He's still a safe distance away when J. puts his hands up, palms outstretched, terror beginning to spread across his face. "No, please, Doug, don't come near me," he says. "Please."

Doug Rader laughs. "Not this time, J.," he says. "Nothing, not a thing. I promise. I just want to give you a piece of gum."

"No you don't. It's a trick. You just want to play a trick on me."

"No J. Look, you see this gum?" He unwraps a fresh piece of gum. And by this time he is very close, nose to nose with poor J. "You want this piece of gum, J.?"

J. says no, no thanks. He is leaning backward to get as far away from Rader as he can.

Whereupon Doug folds the gum up carefully, tucks it into his nostril, the left one, then pulls it out, puts it into his mouth and starts chewing.

J.'s dark eyes cloud over and he starts gagging. He puts his hand over his mouth and dashes into the clubhouse toilet. This time he makes it. The time before, he didn't.

It wasn't long before. Rader had been wandering around the dugout, looking for trouble. He sat down next to J., his eyes on the field. He looked for all the world as though he actually cared what was happening in the game. Meanwhile, he was digging an index finger deeply into his right nostril. Emerging with a quantity of effluence, he carefully wiped it onto J.'s bare arm. J. did one of those deep double takes. He couldn't believe it. As soon as he did, he threw up, right there, on the spot, in the dugout. Of course, we all laughed. Watching a man throw up is hilarious.

Then there was the matter of Joe Pepitone's birthday cake. On the cake was inscribed this fond memento: "Happy Birthday, Joe Pepitone." What else? As is the custom, Pepitone set the cake on the clubhouse table. Happens all the time. Somebody gets a box of cookies from back home, a fan sends a box of candy, you open it, set it on the clubhouse table and anybody who wants to digs in. So this cake is sitting there and Doug Rader says, "I'm going to decorate Joe Pepitone's birthday cake." Nobody paid much attention as Rader picked up the cake and went off with it.

In a short while he was back. Sure enough, the cake was decorated and with the most realistic turd any joke shop ever invented. Naturally everybody laughed, even J. Alou. Terrific fake turd.

It happened, though, that the cake was sitting on the table right next to the pass list and when J. Alou went over to put his name on it, he wrinkled his nose. Sniff, sniff. Suddenly he looked up and screamed, "It's real! It's real! Arrggh!"

All at once everybody was sniffing like a pack of hunting dogs. They didn't want to go near the cake. At the same time, they wanted to test the scent. The odor was beginning to spread through the warm room. It *is* real! The clubhouse emptied as though there was a rattlesnake loose in it.

I admit I had a nasty thought. It was to cut a wedge out of the cake, as though someone had eaten it. This would heighten the illusion that this was only some trick icing. I started cutting, but I couldn't finish. I'm no Jesus Alou, but I didn't have the—what can I call it—courage? I left with everybody else. The clubhouse man disposed of the remains, presumably with a ten-foot pole.

I couldn't resist asking Doug Rader how he had managed the decoration.

"I squatted over it," he said. "Perfect aim."

"Did you have any particular design in mind?"

"Yeah. I was going for a bow. Didn't quite make it."

After *Ball Four* came out Rader was one of the guys who managed to keep a decent perspective. The only things he said about it were funny. Like one time I was taking batting practice against the pitching machine when, as was its wont from time to time, it let go with a high hard one at my head. I went flying into the dirt. "Hah," said Doug Rader. "Even the machine is pissed off at you and your book."

And one time, after I had left baseball, I ran into the club while I was on a book-signing trip to Atlanta. I went to dinner with Rader, Norm Miller and Jack DiLauro. It was a nice dinner. Afterward I dropped them off at their hotel and as the

cab drove off, Rader hollered after me, at the top
of his voice, "YOU DIRTY JAP!"

I'll miss men like Jim Owens. This is what he
said to Norm Miller about me: "He's a hard work-
er. He always gives me a hundred percent. I don't
give a shit what he wrote in that book. All I care
about is his pitching."

Baseball prides itself on having just that attitude. In fact, though, it makes a difference if you
write a book. Or if you're black. Or have a mus-
tache. Or long hair. Or the wrong political opinions. Owens didn't care about anything but the
baseball. He is a rare man.

Oh, and this was his line after *Ball Four* came
out and I was pitching lousy: "You sure you didn't
write that book as a cover-up?"

I'll miss a guy like Jack Billingham, righthanded
pitcher. Billingham was in charge of rumors around
the Houston club. I'd sidle up to him and ask,
"What's the latest?" and he'd say, "Well, there's
always the Norm Miller-for-anybody-in-the-league
trade. You could think about that one for a while."

But this was when he was still a relief pitcher.
When he became a starter he said he had more
time and promised to work up some rumors involving really big names. This spring his biggie
was that Jim Bouton was making a comeback with
the Astros. He was, of course, an artist at his trade.
The highlight of a good rumorman's life, Bil-

lingham always said, was when he saw his rumor get into print. But the pinnacle, the absolute zenith, was to see the rumor come true. He admitted that didn't happen very often. It was nice to contemplate, though.

I'll miss a guy like Jim Pagliaroni, a catcher, and a funny man. Once we were talking about *True Grit*, the motion picture. Pag said he thought he had the best definition of true grit: trying to make it through a hangover without a greenie.

And Gary Bell. Gary's out of baseball now and in the real estate business. I like to think I turned him on to that. Anyway, he was my roommate during a lot of the time I was putting *Ball Four* on tape. And one time, I remember him saying, "You know, Rooms, there's going to be some recriminations about this book." Gary Bell is a perspicacious fellow.

I'll miss not being around when a guy like Tom Griffin of the Astros gets off a line about what losing was like with that club: "We may lose a lot, but when we win it sure is difficult."

I'll even miss Nockahoma. This was the Indian that did a war dance every time somebody on the Atlanta team hit a home run. You could hit him with a stone or a dirt bomb from the bullpen when he came out of his tent. One of these days it's going to be a real bomb. Eventually the times catch up even to baseball players.

I'll miss the kidding in the bullpen about the paranoia of the front office. One of the times we were on a losing streak in Houston, the club started to make a big deal out of the players' weights. The reason we were losing is that we had gained a half pound each, or something. One evening there was a phone call in the bullpen and Fred Gladding, who was overweight even when we were winning, said: "It's Spec Richardson [the general manager]. He says Doug Rader looks overweight on his television set."

Another thing I'll treasure—the bus songs. The one about Joe Pepitone, sung, of course, to the tune of "Yankee Doodle":

> I'm a Yankee Doodle Dandy,
> Yankee Doodle do or die,
> A real lefthander with a head to match,
> I am a real sweetie pie.
> Booze and broads are what I live for,
> Baseball's really not my bag.
> Yankee Doodle came to Houston
> Acting like a phony,
> I am that Yankee Doodle fag.

And the one about what'sizname, to the tune of "If You Knew Susie":

If you knew Bouton
Like we know Bouton,
Oh boy, is he a Jap.
What he calls candor
Is just plain slander,
He'll stab the back
Of anyone who swings a bat.
He'll wreck your marriage,
These are the facts;
And brag about his royalties
And movie contracts.
He thinks it's funny,
But it's blood money;
Oh boy, what a Jap.

I'll miss the organist at Wrigley Field in Chicago. Every time Harry Walker came out on the field, "I'm Just Wild About Harry" would be played. After *Ball Four* I got my own special song. It was "I Wonder Who's Kissing Her Now."

I was furious with Ed Vargo, the umpire. My knuckleball was moving pretty good, but it was just missing the corners. At least Vargo said it was missing. I guess he was right. Still, I was furious at him for not calling even one of them a strike. Afterward I remembered Whitey Ford's favorite Ryne Duren story. Duren was the wild-man relief pitcher who had a couple of great years with the Yankees. Anyway, on this day he was throwing

BBs, all of them neck high. Four straight, to three straight batters. Finally he walked across a run and he stormed up to the home-plate umpire. "Goddammit, where the hell are those pitches?"

"Right up here, Ryne," the umpire said, pointing to his neck.

"Well, goddammit," Duren said, "I've got to have that pitch."

The games we played in the bullpen. Like Mr. Science. Tom Griffin was usually Mr. Science.

Q. What is the sun made of?

MR. SCIENCE: Two things; heat and light.

Q. How do you find the radius of a circle?

MR. SCIENCE: Measure it, dummy.

Q. Why do birds fly?

MR. SCIENCE: They'd never get anywhere if they had to walk.

And Unknown Facts of History.

GRIFFIN: You know who Paul Revere was, don't you?

ME: Yeah, he told everybody the British were coming.

GRIFFIN: Right. But actually he wasn't Paul Revere. His right name was Tommy Rothblatt.

ME: Then why was he called Paul Revere?

GRIFFIN: Because, dummy, would you buy Rothblattware? And who the hell would ever write a poem about the midnight ride of Tommy Rothblatt?

And Promotion. There were nights when there were too many empty seats in the Astrodome. We knew what to do about it.

"Midgets," Tom Griffin said. "People will pay to see midgets."

"Not unless they're doing something," Norm Miller said.

"How about dropping them from the roof in parachutes?" I said.

"Not exciting enough," Griffin said. "How about nine midgets, one an inning, and only eight parachutes?"

"We could sell it as a raffle," Miller said. "The fans who drew the midget without the parachute would get a prize."

"Great," Griffin said. "We could call it Dollars for Midgets."

And Obituaries That Would Be Fun to Read.

"That's the last time I buy an iron lung at Kresge's," said the widow of John P. Barnapuss.

Mrs. Irma Smedley, Mrs. Harriet Cholera and Mrs. Bernice Barnacle will be needing a fourth at bridge as the result of the death of Mrs. Georgiana Peachtree.

Until his recent vacation in northern India, the late Jonathan C. Farnsworth had always insisted there were no man-eating tigers.

If you don't believe that you try to hold on to stuff like that, how do you explain that one of the first things I did once I was out of baseball was make a comeback as a semi-pro pitcher. Yes, I did. The team? Trenton Pavers by name. The game was in Bridgeton, New Jersey.

Don't think I wasn't nervous. It was a big game. One more loss and the Pavers would be out of the tournament. You don't go into a crucial situation like that lightly. In fact, right before I set out for the game my wife said, "Isn't it nice not to worry about how you do in the ball game?"

Sure. And when she kissed me good-by, she said, "Give me a call and let me know how you did." It's the same thing she used to say when I pitched for the Yankees.

On the way to the game I stopped off at a sporting goods shop to pick up a cup and some sanitary socks. The lady in the store gave me some funny looks. "Those things don't go big down here," she said. "How about a fishing rod?"

There was no clubhouse, of course. I dressed in somebody's office across the street from the field. Most of the guys put their uniforms on at home and drove to the park dressed. Somebody found a Little League cup for me, but I wouldn't wear it, and not only because it was uncomfortable. I have my pride, you know.

The game was against a team called the Washington Black Sox, an all-black club that, it was said, once beat the Baltimore Orioles in an exhibition game. The only thing that happened all evening that I didn't thoroughly enjoy was a fat man in a yellow shirt coming up to me and saying, "Send these niggers back where they came from." I wished I was more like Gene Brabender, who once said to me, "Where I come from we only argue for a little while. Then we start to hit."

Actually, there was something else I didn't altogether enjoy. Warming up. It was incredible. Three weeks out of the game, and in the first minute of warming up I pulled a groin muscle and hurt my pitching elbow. It felt like somebody had set a fire under it.

The first instruction I got was about the clock. "Don't tell me, I know," I said. "Any ball hit off the clock is a home run." I was right. Somebody hit the clock off me and sure enough, it was a home run. Except the clock was more than that. It was a twenty-second clock. It measured the time between pitches and you were allowed only twenty seconds. Otherwise you got a called ball. I got so involved I had two balls called on me. Boy, those guys are sticklers for rules.

I had to abandon my knuckleball early on. I'd strike a guy out on three great ones and then I'd get hammered with three straight hits off bad ones. I ended up with the fastball, scattering a mere thirteen hits. (Well, I *told* you these guys once beat the Orioles.) I walked only two, struck out ten and every time the manager passed me, he'd pat me on the ass. Funny thing, he mumbled the same sort of phrases at me that big league managers did. "Get that first hitter now." I mean, what for? Why not walk the first hitter and get the next three?

Anyway, we won 7–5, and the manager was so pleased he asked me if I wanted to come down the next night and coach at first base. What the hell, it was only a three-hour drive from my home. If you love the game . . . Well, I do. Only not quite that much. I explained I had other commitments. Maybe I should have gone, though. Without me to guide their first-base fortunes the Pavers lost and were eliminated. Ah, I couldn't have come back anyway. I was so sore I could barely move out of bed.

At any rate, it was a sweet scene and I enjoyed every moment. Like I was sitting on the bench, hot and sweaty, after warming up, and I asked if anybody had a towel. No one did. So a policeman who was standing behind the screen heard me, jumped into his car, drove home, picked up a towel and brought it back to me. All I could tell him was thanks.

And during the game there was this bit. One of the baseballs was fouled off against the fence and there was a big gash torn in the cover, right down to the yarn. The ball was thrown around the infield and the third baseman called the umpire's attention to the tear. Naturally, the ball was taken out of play. It would never have happened that way in a big league game. The ball would have been thrown to the pitcher and he'd have been able to throw it for at least one hellacious strike.

It would be wrong to conclude, I think, that there is more honesty in semi-pro baseball than major league. Alas, I put it down to ignorance.

Another thing I enjoyed during the game was the chatter. The players kept throwing one-liners at me from the book.

"Smoke 'em inside."

"Check the rack on that broad."

"Beaver at twelve o'clock."

And after we won, they all crowded around like it was a World Series. Despite the pain, it was beautiful.

After the game I sat down in the ticket booth and signed autographs. I must have signed about thirty books and a couple of hundred pieces of paper, popcorn boxes and programs. The mayor and the city councilmen, among the multitude of 5,000, came over to say hello, and a great good time was had by all, especially me.

So if you really want to know what I planned to do with my spare time this summer, my first out of baseball, it was to play semi-professional baseball. I've got the team picked out. They're called the Ridgewood-Paramus Barons, and I've got my application in. I hear there's only one problem. I may not be good enough.

I was in Atlanta for a book-signing on September 25 and the Houston club was in town. I went to the game that night, wandered out into right field and sat down on a seat at the edge of the bullpen. I could hear the guys talking, making fun of one of the umpires, telling dirty stories; Jimmy Ray and Jack DiLauro were throwing stones into a paper cup. And there I was, dressed in a suit and a tie. I felt like an outsider, and at the same time I felt so close to those men it was as though I were still in the bullpen, as though I *belonged* there. A wave of nostalgia swept over me and all I wanted to do was jump down into the bullpen and put a uniform on, sit on the bench, laugh.

When Norm Miller came to bat, I forgot I was on the outside. I said, "C'mon, Rooms." I said it out loud, and then I looked around to see if anybody had heard. I felt foolish and alone. Then Wade Blasingame spotted me. He looked up and said, "How you doing, Jim? Getting by, are you?" That broke everybody up. Me too. And Fred Gladding said, "Watch out, you guys. He may still be taking notes."

After that, it was just terrific. A lot of the guys came over, climbed up on the tarpaulin, sat down and shot the shit. There was the teasing, of course. "You seen Mickey Mantle yet?" And the usual friendly questions. "You like your new job?" "How are the kids?" I was grinning so broadly my face hurt.

Jim Owens invited me into the clubhouse after the game. I'd asked him if anything funny had happened recently and he said, "Well, we lost the hot dogs in L.A. the other night." He meant Harry had banned the frankfurters after the game. Must have been a bad loss.

I felt awkward about going into the clubhouse. "You sure Harry won't mind?" I said. "Hell no," Owens said.

So I went in and sat down next to Doug Rader (who promptly described the game, won by the Astros, as a "semi ball-buster"), and pretty soon there was a half-circle of chairs around us. Even Harry Walker came over and sat down. Within a half hour he was giving me batting tips.

Later on I went out to dinner with DiLauro, Miller and Rader. That's the night Rader called me "DIRTY JAP!" and I went up to my room feeling happy and sad and, at the very last, miserable.

There are feelings I will never have again. I'll never again hang out in a bullpen. I'll never again sit on the bench all alone before a World Series game, looking casual while praying inside that I won't disgrace myself; looking bored while being able to count my own heartbeats, looking cool while feeling the hot clamps on my belly. I know that beating the team that once, maybe, beat the Orioles in an exhibition game will never be the same as getting Henry Aaron out four times in a game, or Harmon Killebrew. I know I've given up a great deal.

At the same time, I can't help laughing a lot. I wake up in the morning with a smile on my face. I've got a new career. I've got the kind of financial security a guy with my talents could never have earned in baseball. And when I walk in the street, people say, "Hey, that's Jim Bouton." There are few people in this world, I tell you, who can scratch so many basic itches in their lives, including the underlying ham.

I think, sometimes, these days, about one of the first managers I had in baseball. He used to like to tell us that there were three ways to get out of this wonderful game. He said you could drink your way out, you could eat your way out, or you could fuck your way out. You can also, I believe, write your way out.

And when I'm thinking of all the things that went into my leaving this game to which I had brought so much energy and love, I think of something my daughter Laurie said not long ago, when she was four. We were on our way from Houston to our home in New Jersey with a stop to visit Bobbie's folks in Michigan. In the crush, one of Laurie's favorite dolls was mislaid. Bobbie tried to comfort her. The doll, she said, had been sent home with a lot of our other things. And Laurie said, "Home? Which home?"

From now on, she'll know. It will be good for all of us.

BALL FOUR

by Jim Bouton
Edited by Leonard Shecter

In 1963 Jim Bouton won 21 games for the Yankees. In 1964 he won 18 games and lost two in the world series. Then Bouton lost his fast-ball and came to the gut-twisting decision to try to make it with the knuckleball —the most erratic and difficult pitch there is!

Bouton got sent to the minors and fought his way back to the majors. Almost wrecked himself working on his knuckleball. Insulted people. Made enemies. Made friends. Never gave up. And wrote a book.

BALL FOUR—the biggest bestseller ever published about baseball and the men who play it!

"Very likely the funniest book of the year"
—*The New Yorker*

A DELL BOOK $1.25